Netherlandish Scrolled Gables
of the Sixteenth and
Early Seventeenth Centuries

The publication of this monograph
has been aided by a grant from the
Samuel H. Kress Foundation

Dordrecht, Rietdijksche Poort, 1590, from an eighteenth-century watercolor

HENRY-RUSSELL HITCHCOCK

Netherlandish Scrolled Gables
of the Sixteenth and
Early Seventeenth Centuries

PUBLISHED BY

NEW YORK UNIVERSITY PRESS

for the College Art Association of America

NEW YORK 1978

Monographs on Archaeology and Fine Arts
sponsored by
THE ARCHAEOLOGICAL INSTITUTE OF AMERICA
and
THE COLLEGE ART ASSOCIATION OF AMERICA
XXXIV
Editor:
Isabelle Hyman

Library of Congress Cataloging in Publication Data
Hitchcock, Henry-Russell, 1903–
    Netherlandish scrolled gables of the sixteenth and early
seventeenth centuries.

    (Monographs on archaeology and fine arts; 34)
    1. Gables—Netherlands—Influence.   2. Gables—Europe,
Northern.   3. Architecture, Renaissance—Netherlands.
4. Architecture, Renaissance—Europe, Northern.   I. College
Art Association of America.   II. Title.   III. Series.
NA2920.H57   721'.5   77-81905
ISBN 0-8147-3383-2

To the memory of my ancestors
the Pilgrim Fathers
who left Holland in 1620
and settled the Plymouth Colony

Contents

Preface

SINCE Colen Campbell, in the first quarter of the eighteenth century, brought out the English translation of Palladio's *Quattro libri*, the architecture of Renaissance Italy has been a recurrent subject especially dear to architects and scholars writing in English. The flood of such publications by Americans as well as by the British did not diminish in the third quarter of the twentieth century, nor does it bid fair to do so in the near future. A major work by two continental scholars, Heydenreich and Lotz, moreover, made its original appearance lately in a Pelican volume in English, not in German. As regards French Renaissance architecture, from the books of Ward and Blomfield early in this century to Blunt's current Pelican volume, English scholars have made notable contributions outbalancing at times the production of French writers.

Very different is the situation for northern Europe: in Germany, in the Low Countries, and in Scandinavia. The best book on later Dutch architecture in English is by a Briton, Katherine Fremantle, on the *Baroque Town Hall of Amsterdam*. But, as the title indicates, her main subject comes late in the Renaissance story, indeed after its end. For Denmark there is also an important work in English, Skovgaard's *A King's Architecture*, dealing with the work done, earlier than the period of the Amsterdam Town Hall, for Christian IV and almost entirely by architects of Netherlandish origin.

In the Pelican series, the volumes on *Dutch Art and Architecture* and on that of Belgium give little space to buildings, while none of the series covers the Renaissance architecture of the central German lands. Such a work this author has for sometime had in hand. The present book is devoted to one aspect of the architecture Netherlanders were responsible for in their homelands and had carried, by the third quarter of the sixteenth century, northward to Denmark and eastward along the Baltic. It precedes the publication of that on the German Renaissance.

This book does not offer a complete account of Netherlandish architecture of the sixteenth and early seventeenth centuries, nor even a balanced one. It deals with a particular, and usually dominating, feature of what Netherlanders were building at home and carrying abroad over much of northern Europe from 1520, or a little before, down to 1620 and a little after.

The analysis of northern gable design, including cross-reference to parallel developments in Germany, is frankly physiognomic. There is no attempt to discuss plans, although it is obvious that the buildings are predominantly of narrow rectangular shape, with their high roofs at a right angle to the street—or, if broader, with a central cross-gable or a range of gabled dormers of brick or stone—and more usually with party walls rather than freestanding. The particular structure of the gabled facades—interestingly, the Dutch word for a front elevation is *gevel* (gable)—is not discussed, because its character is so evident, beyond the predominance throughout all the regions that are touched on of brick as the basic building material. Brick is supplemented in varying degrees, however, even in the northern Netherlands—which is usually, if incorrectly, called Holland—with imported freestone which was transported by water. Though stone could be used for lintels over windows, more usually semi-elliptical arches of brick, of a sort inherited from the Late Gothic, or flat arches were used to cap them. Evidence of the exaggerated importance of gables is the way they are sometimes carried quite a bit higher than the tall roofs they front so that their crowns have to be braced from the rear by diagonal iron struts.

Though this is hardly a picture-book like Timmer's splendidly illustrated *Dutch Art and Life*, the pictures—not by any means alone the photographs of extant work, but the old drawings and watercolors of buildings that have been destroyed or modified—must provide the particular interest of the book. Happily, in several cases, from the pre-Renaissance town hall of Gent to the late-sixteenth-century one of Leiden, it has been possible to include some architects' drawings, the more interesting because the executed work diverges so much from what was projected.

The prime purpose of the author has been to bring together a varied array of decorated gables from all the regions where Netherlandish craftsmen worked at home and abroad and to arrange them chronologically, so that the linkage of northern Renaissance design from London on the west to Copenhagen on the north and Gdańsk to the east will be apparent. Most important in the preparation of the book was the assistance of the Rijksdienst voor de Monumentenzorg in Zeist and the Kunsthistorisch Instituut of the University of Utrecht, the official Belgian photographic archive A.C.L. in Brussels, the Instytut Sztuki in Warsaw, the Royal Library in Copenhagen, and the Bildarchiv of the University of Marburg. Other sources, from which only one or two illustrations were chosen, are indicated in the list of illustrations by abbreviated credits, some to sources, but mostly to photographers.

As regards dating and attributions, I have accepted what are given in the latest publications in the various countries. Happily, in this period a great many buildings, particularly in Holland, carry the date of construction on the facade. The more serious problems of attribution, from the question of who was the responsible designer of the Palais de Savoie at Mechelen in Belgium early in the period to the Frederiksborg Slot at Hillerød in Denmark toward its end, are discussed in the text with only the most probable entered in the captions under the illustrations.

The analysis of gable design depends more on examination of the buildings, almost all of which I know at first hand if they are extant, than on earlier studies. All the same, I have had the advantage of assistance, mostly by correspondence, from various scholars. I would like to mention particularly Dr. B. Rebel of Utrecht, now of the University of Amsterdam, who drove me in his car all over Holland and parts of Belgium several years ago, Dr. Dambre-Van Tyghem of the University of Gent, John Harris of the R.I.B.A. Drawings Collection and Sir John Summerson of the Soane Museum in London, with both of whom I have had most profitable discussions of Inigo Jones's possible continental sources—not Dutch, Harris and I suspect, but German.

No one can be more aware than this author of how much remains to be done in the study of Northern Renaissance architecture before our understanding of it, not in terms of particular national regions, but internationally, catches up with our knowledge of the period in Italy or even in France. The attempt here has been to correlate geographically the story of prominent features from the later portion of Kirby Hall in Northamptonshire in England of the 1570s or 1580s to the Great Arsenal in Gdańsk in Poland of the early years of the seventeenth century. The first is either by a Netherlandish craftsman or by a native English one who drew his ideas from Antwerp publications; the latter is by a Netherlander from Mechelen whose career had begun in the late 1570s with the casing in stone of Slot Kronborg at Helsingør (Elsinore) in Denmark. I hope this will encourage other students of Renaissance architecture to break away from exclusive preoccupation with southern Europe into broad studies of this period in the north. Such should supplement the more antiquarian local studies that already exist in great quantity and will eventually produce a better coordinated art-historical whole.

It is gratifying, in this connection, that I have had the continuing assistance of two former students, William G. Foulks and Mosette Broderick, who have worked with me both on this book and that on German Renaissance architecture, which has been in parallel preparation though this has first reached the printer. Both Mr. Foulks and Mrs. Broderick are associated with Columbia University though they took courses with me at the Institute of Fine Arts and Mr. Foulks has occasionally assisted me there. Thanks to their association with Columbia and exceptional knowledge of the resources of the Avery Library, they were both in a position to do research, bibliographical particularly, as my surrogates in the Avery Library. This paragraph can only suggest the breadth and the depth of my indebtedness to them both.

List of Illustrations

The illustrations do not appear in strictly sequential order
since they follow the sequence of text references.

XIII

I Introduction

IN 1638 the dowager queen of France, Henri IV's widow Marie de Médicis, who had been exiled to Brussels in 1631, made an entrée into Amsterdam. That great mercantile port had risen to primacy over Antwerp with the blocking by the Dutch of the River Schelde and, thus, of Antwerp's access to the sea.[1] The city the queen saw (Fig. 1) was very different in its architecture from that cradle of the Italian Renaissance, Florence, where this daughter of Grand Duke Francesco de' Medici had been brought up. Dearest to her heart was the Pitti Palace, of which she had had drawings made to provide a model—not very closely followed by her architect—for the Luxembourg Palace she called on Salomon de Brosse to build and Rubens to decorate.

The full triumph of what is often called Dutch Palladian lay still a decade ahead: Jacob van Campen began the grandiose Amsterdam *Raadhuis* (town hall), later the Royal Palace,[2] in 1648. She could, however, have seen and admired the advanced style of the small but palatial *Mauritshuis*, newly erected in The Hague by him and Pieter Post. Dating from 1633, this was built for a member of the all-but-royal house of Orange, Johan Maurits van Nassau. Even the latest gabled houses of the burghers of Amsterdam (Fig. 4), on the other hand, were still very different from French urban building in the Place Royale—today the Place des Vosges—and the Place Dauphine in Paris, which her husband had commissioned at the opening of the century. The continuous horizontal cornices and hipped roofs of the French houses, not to speak of their severely restrained detail, had as yet only a very few parallels in the cities of the Netherlands.

Not much survives, however, of the gabled Amsterdam that had been so extensively built up during the previous half-century. Today that Amsterdam can best be pictured, otherwise than from paintings, engravings, and drawings, not in any Dutch city, but in two very large squares that survive, effectively intact, at Arras in northern France. This prosperous place, once so famous for its tapestries, had long been ruled by the counts of Flanders; it became a part of France only in 1640, after five years of war, and suffered a great deal more damage—plausibly repaired half a century ago—in World War I.[3] There one double facade of the early sixteenth century, with pointed arches below and linked gables of stepped outline above, still stands at the closed end of the Place des Marchés (Fig. 2). But the other gables in this square, as well as those in the nearby one before the Hotel de Ville and along the connecting street, are all framed by scrolling, from such later sixteenth-century examples as flank the above-mentioned Gothic facade to innumerable others, many of which are certainly of eighteenth-century date (Fig. 3) and only a few before 1640 or even 1679.

These squares in Arras with their ranges of nearly identical scrolled gables, of which only the legally enforced regularity is French, contrast with the provincial version of the Place Royale at the center of the *fiat* city of Charleville in the same border region, farther to the east in the Ardennes.[4] Today this borderland in northern France lies just to the south of Belgium and Luxemburg. Thus it extends, west to east, from the Pas de Calais at the inner end of the English Channel to the Moselle River where it flows out of France. In the sixteenth and seventeenth centuries this was a major section of the frontier between the Netherlandish territories, of which the Habsburg Emperor Maximilian I had early obtained control by his marriage to Mary of Burgundy, and the royal French territories of the Valois. But it is more relevant here that the region marks a significant cultural frontier in western Europe between the north and the south, like Switzerland to the south and east or Alsace in between.[5]

There are notable differences between north and south in all fields, some of which will soon be noted. Moreover, the builders of these squares at Charleville and Arras were socially distinct: in the one case, a prince, Charles de Gonzague, duc de Nevers; in the other, members of a mercantile oligarchy. The distinction is not insignificant. The patronage of greater princes than Charles de Gonzague, such as the Emperor Ferdinand I in Prague in the middle decades of the sixteenth century[6] and the Danish builder-king Christian IV following 1600 (Figs. 90, 106–108), was already exceptional in northern Europe, though it would become important once more in the later seventeenth century. Not Elizabeth I but her subjects were the ambitious patrons of architecture in the England[7] of this period (Figs. 67, 68).

From the *Groote Markt* of Antwerp (Fig. 66) to the *Długi Targ* (Fig. 54) in Gdańsk (Danzig),[8] the erection of secular buildings of any architectural pretension in the principal squares of the cities of the sixteenth and early seventeenth centuries was for the most part sponsored publicly by city councils or by merchants' guilds and privately by prosperous

burghers. Such a patronage was definitely middle class and, like that of the English mag-
nates, rarely extended to the employment of imported Italians. Princes, on the other hand,
often called to the north craftsmen from Italy either as designers or as executants—Ferdinand in Bohemia and other Habsburgs in the southern Austrian duchies or the Wittelsbach
Duke Ludwig IX of Bavaria[9]—to project and to carry out buildings. Alternatively, richly
decorated suites of interiors were commissioned, such as those for which Zygmunt III Vasa,
for example, in Poland employed the Italian-Swiss Giovanni Trevano from Lugano. These
were therefore likely to be distinctly southern, not northern, in character.[10]

As regards interiors, however, Hans Fugger of Augsburg, an international banker, easily
rivaled in the north contemporary princes as a client for Italians. Indeed, he even supplied
William IX with the team of Italian-trained artists the Bavarian duke employed first at
Landshut and then in Munich. It had been an earlier Fugger, moreover, Jakob "der Reiche,"
who was responsible for the earliest Italianate architecture in Germany, even if that did not
follow for a decade or more after the initial employment of Italian craftsmen by one prince
in Hungary, already in the last quarter of the 15th century, and others in Bohemia and in
Poland around 1500.

A characteristic difference between the north and the south was in religion, although one
should not exaggerate the importance of this for secular architecture. But the Protestant
Reform began in the north, never penetrating far into the south, and the middle-class
patrons of urban architecture in the north were usually Protestants, not Catholics. Even if
under Catholic rule, they were considerably less responsive to the codified architectural
doctrine of sixteenth-century Italy than were some, at least, of the princes. In church architecture the considerable disparity between the Paduan Bernardo Morando's church of the
1580s at Zamość in Catholic Poland and such slightly later Protestant edifices as de Brosse's
second Huguenot Temple at Charenton outside Paris or the church the Lutheran Duke
Friedrich of Württemberg had his German architect Schweikhardt build for Baptist refugees
from Calvinist Holland[11] in his exclave Montbéliard—to name two examples that are both
in France—is not irrelevant. All three, however, may be considered exceptional. Changes of
religion—first one way in the mid-sixteenth century, then the other after 1600—had only a
slight effect on the *Schlosskapelle* (castle chapel) and the *Hofkirche* (court-church) of the
Wittelsbach rulers of the Upper Palatinate in Neuburg-a.-d.-Donau. Indeed, even the
grandest and most advanced early Jesuit church in the north, St. Michael in Munich of the
1580s and 1590s, though largely—perhaps entirely—designed by the Italian-trained Dutch
artist Friedrich (Frederik or Federigo) Sustris for William IX, to whom he had earlier been
sent by Hans Fugger, has rather less in common with Vignola's Gesú in Rome than with the
newly built Protestant Münster at Klagenfurt in Carinthia, which was only taken over by
the Jesuits after 1600.

But this book is not much concerned with religious architecture. Certain northern

Protestant churches of the early seventeenth century, from the Hofkirche in Neuburg and those at Bückeburg and Wolfenbüttel in Germany to several for the Calvinists of Amsterdam in Holland, rival in size if not in splendor the most grandiose Jesuit edifices of the early seventeenth century in the north, from the Sint Carolus Borromeus-kerk in Antwerp to the Himmelfahrt Mariä in Cologne.[12] But middle-class secular architecture is, throughout the north of Europe, more typical of this period, even if much building was also carried out for such princely patrons as the electors of Saxony and of the Palatinate in Germany and for King Frederik II of Denmark and his successor, Christian IV. These princes, in any case, were all four Protestants, as were many others who were active patrons of architecture.

In politics and religion there was also considerable disparity between the southern and the northern Netherlands. But the cultural center of gravity, if one may put it so, was shifting from Catholic Antwerp and the provinces of Brabant and Flanders in the south—today the better part of western Belgium—to Protestant Amsterdam and the Dutch provinces to the north. As a whole these are usually thought of as Holland by foreigners, but most correctly they are called Nederland or, in English, the Netherlands. In this book, however, the term "Netherlands" is used to cover both north and south.

Interest in the study of Italian Renaissance architecture did not diminish in the middle decades of this century. Research and publication continued at a high level as scholars from all over the Western world examined in minute detail various aspects of building production in Italy and by Italians active elsewhere in the fifteenth and sixteenth centuries. But there was no parallel increase in relevant interest in the Renaissance architecture of the north; what there was, moreover, tended to be of a regional and antiquarian nature rather than broadly art-historical.

As regards the gradual increase in the authority of architect-designers in the sixteenth century, the change proceeded more rapidly in the south than in the north of Europe.[13] It is by no means impossible, nor even particularly tendentious, to tell the story of Italian Renaissance architecture in the sixteenth century as a series of overlapping accounts of the *oeuvres* of individual architects from Bramante to Maderno. To attempt to do the same in the Netherlands would be pointless as architect-designers had as yet no comparable autonomy. All the same, Rombout Keldermans, a *bouwmeester* (master builder) of Brabant, could already produce by the second decade of the century elaborate elevational drawings (Fig. 7) of projected structures that are more professional looking to modern eyes than those of Lieven de Key two generations later (Figs. 78, 80), if not those of Hendrick de Keyser at least as his are known at second hand from the engravings in the posthumous publication of his works, *Architectura moderna*, Amsterdam, 1631.

Guyot de Beaugrant, Kelderman's associate on the Palais de Savoie late in the second decade of the sixteenth century was primarily a sculptor, not a designing architect, as was also Cornelis Floris, who was responsible for the two major Antwerp buildings of the 1560s, the Raadhuis and the *Hanseaten Huis* (headquarters of the German merchants), as well as for elaborate tombs in several parts of northern Europe. But, for that matter, in Italy Raphael—if not to the same degree his pupil Giulio Romano—is certainly better known for his paintings than for his buildings.

From those trained as masons who were in most cases the actual bouwmeesters to city officials without much relevant experience, plenty of names survive of men associated in one way or another with construction, and presumably with the architectural designing that preceded it. Neither Jan Wallot nor Christian Sixdeniers, who were responsible for the *Griffie* (chancery) (Fig. 25) at Brugge (Bruges), were architects in the Italian Renaissance sense. There is little more assurance that the *patroon* (design) Joos Rooman provided for the masons to follow on such a proto-Academic facade as that of the Bollaertskamer (Fig. 71) in Gent (Ghent) in the 1580s was any more precise than Rombout Keldermans's and Domien de Waghemaekere's elevations for the earlier portion of the Gent *Raadhuis* (town hall) next door when they projected it two generations earlier (Fig. 7). It is evident, moreover, that Lieven de Key's elevations of the 1590s for the *Raadhuis* and the *Rijnlandshuis* in Leiden (Figs. 78, 80) were drastically modified when they were carried out by others.

The Renaissance architecture of the Netherlands is less anonymous outside its homelands since the employment of foreigners was usually documented abroad. The work of Anthonis van Opbergen, both in Denmark and at Gdańsk (Figs. 63, 77, 91, 92), implies that he had a recognized professional competence not rivaled by that of the master builders and master masons who stayed home and worked in Holland or in Brabant and Flanders. First in Emden and then in Denmark, several generations of Steenwinckels from the Netherlands are identifiable, as also of Van den Blockes in Gdańsk. All the same, despite the international influence of the published plates of ornament by Cornelis Floris and Jan Vredeman de Fries (Figs. 34, 35, 38, 47), including in the case of the latter actual designs for scrolled gables (Fig. 48), there is no northern architectural literature of the sixteenth century to compare with the publications of Serlio, Vignola, and Palladio. To learn about it one must turn to the studies of modern scholars.

In the place of a formal bibliography, some indication of the existing twentieth-century literature, with comments on its relative usefulness, may be introduced here. Scholars, particularly Germans, noted early the linkage between Renaissance production in various parts of northern Europe. Gustav Glück, *Die Kunst der Renaissance in Deutschland, den Niederlanden, Frankreich . . .*, Berlin [1928] in the Propyläen Kunstgeschichte included not only the Netherlands (in the broader sense) and even France, but also other northern realms, quite as did, twenty years before, G. G. von Bezold, *Die Baustile*, in A. Kroner, *Handbuch der Architektur*, 7. Band, Leipzig, 1908, a work that also covered, in addition to the German lands, Holland, Belgium, and Denmark. Further evidence of the recognition early in this century of the close connections that existed, not least toward the end of the Renaissance period in the early seventeenth century, is the Dutch scholar D. F. Slothouwer's *Bouwkunst der Nederlandsche Renaissance in Denemarken*, Amsterdam, 1924. This may be contrasted to the more extended treatment of the subject by J. A. Skovgaard, writing in English, in *A King's Architecture: Christian IV and his Buildings*, London [1973]. Broader in its treatment of Netherlandish influence abroad is C. Horst, *Die Architektur der Renaissance in den Niederlanden und ihre Austrahlungen*, The Hague, 1930, while W. Sahner, *Die Architektur Deutschlands und der Niederlande in ihrer Wechselbeziehungen* [?1956] is more limited in scope.

No scholar, in any case, disputes the fact that Northern Renaissance design was transmitted both by books of ornament, prepared and published in Antwerp from the mid-sixteenth century on, and by Netherlandish craftsmen recurrently employed after that in various parts of northern Europe. These were in many cases, it may be presumed, Protestants in flight from religious persecution in the southern Netherlands not, like their predecessors before the Reformation, called to work abroad primarily because of their international artistic reputation. This situation has a broad stylistic relevance long recognized by foreigners though somewhat neglected, except for Slothouwer, by the Netherlanders themselves, as the publications just listed clearly indicate.

Relevant Dutch literature, of which Slothouwer's book is an excellent example less heavily slanted toward urbanism than are most, is more profuse than Belgian and may be discussed first. The most extensive general coverage for Holland is still provided by F. A. J. Vermeulen in his *Handboek tot de Geschiedenis der Nederlandsche Bouwkunst*, 3 vols., The Hague, 1928–41, which had appeared originally in many parts beginning in 1923. But there are earlier works of interest in connection with the study of the scrolled gable. For example, two illustrations used in this book, Figs. 4 and 101, were taken from the book of A. W. Weissman, *Het Amsterdamsche Woonhuis van 1500–1800*, Amsterdam [1885], otherwise devoted to interiors. The date is of some consequence. Weissman's book reflects in Holland a particular sort of historical interest evident elsewhere in the popularity, with both architects and public, of Northern Renaissance models both in the Germany of the Bismarck period and in what the Victorians called Pont Street Dutch, an alien aspect of the "Queen Anne" in contemporary England. Indeed, H. P. Berlage in his entries in the first competition of the 1880s for the Amsterdam *Beurs* (exchange) echoed the Dutch architecture of around 1600 in a rather similar way. Another much later work by the well-traveled Amsterdam city architect Weissman, who had even been to the United States, *Geschiedenis der Nederlandsche bouwkunst . . .*, Amsterdam, 1912, is more general. Long after that came J. Godefroy's *Geschiedenis van der Bouwkunst in Nederland . . .*, Amsterdam [1920].

Ozinga's book on church architecture of 1929 has already been mentioned in Note 12.

Among late works dealing with the northern Netherlands the *Kunstreisboek voor Neder-land*, Amsterdam, 1965, is most useful, distinctly more so than J. Rosenberg, S. Slive, and E. H. ter Kuile, *Dutch Art and Architecture 1600–1800*, Harmondsworth [1966]. Though more accessible since it is in English, this begins much too late. For the mid-seventeenth century, a much superior work, Miss Fremantle's book, also in English, which focuses on the Amsterdam Town Hall, was referenced in Note 2. Among those who worked on the *Kunstreisboek* in addition to ter Kuile was Ozinga, and many others contributed in the various provinces, but the authority is joint, not individual, as regards the particular entries.

As all the Dutch buildings to be described and discussed below are covered by the *Kunstreisboek*, very few specific page references to it are given in the Notes. Instead, since it is organized not alphabetically but by provinces, the province is noted for each town in which particular monuments are located.

Brief but equally authoritative and in English is [H. E. van Gelder], *Guide to Dutch Art*, 3d rev. ed., The Hague, 1961. There is also the English translation of J. J. Timmer, *A History of Dutch Life and Art* [London], 1959, dealing with architecture on pp. 87–123. This is a picture book, but has excellent chapters of text.

The classic work of Vermeulen was of particular help in finding relevant buildings while visiting Dutch towns and cities, but later references have been preferred for the Notes in this book.

For the southern Netherlands, that is, Belgium today, only a few books need be listed. The earliest of consequence is P. Parent, *L'Architecture des Pays-Bas meridionaux aux XVIe, XVIIe et XVIIIe siècles*, Paris-Brussels, 1926. Then there is O. Vande Castyne, *L'Architecture privée en Belgique dans les centres urbains aux XVIe et XVIIe siècles*, Brussels, 1932, a general work, and also more specialized books devoted to particular regions such as F. Courtoy, *L'Architecture civile dans le Namurois aux XVIIe et XVIIIe siècles* and *Antwerpen die Scone*, particularly vol. V: *Oude gildehuizen en ambrachtshuizen* [Antwerp], 1972, with text by L. de Barsée. Another author is Stan Leurs. His restricted *Kunstgeschiedenis der Bouwkunst in Vlaanderen*, Antwerp, 1946, was later superseded by the more extensive contributions he provided concerning architecture in J. Duverger, ed., *Kunstgeschiedenis der Nederlanden*, 3d ed., Utrecht, 1956. Much of this Belgian literature is in Flemish, and none is in English.

For the early introduction of Renaissance architectural elements both in the north and in the south in painting, sculpture, stained glass, and church accessories there is an account in C. Horst, *Die Architektur der Renaissance in den Niederlanden . . .*, 1ste Abteilung, 1ste Teil: *Architektur in der Malerei und Innenarchitektur*, The Hague, 1950. Closest to work at fully architectural scale are the tombs and screens in churches. Many of these, mostly of the second half of the century, were commissioned by German and Danish clients.

Especially useful for reference is the *Gids voor de Kunst in België*, Utrecht-Antwerp, 1963, by R. Lemaire and others, which is similar in its coverage to the *Kunstreisboek* for Holland. In English there are only H. Gerson and E. H. ter Kuile, *Art and Architecture in Belgium: 1600–1800*, Harmondsworth [1960], and I. Vandevivere, *Renaissance Art in Belgium: Architecture, Monumental Art*, Brussels, 1973, neither of them of great consequence as regards architecture. For the contemporary work of painters and sculptors associated with architecture, both in the northern and in the southern Netherlands, G. von der Osten and H. Vey, *Painting and Sculpture in Germany and the Netherlands 1500–1600*, Baltimore [1969], is more valuable, supplementing Horst's book of 1950.

The story of Renaissance architecture in the north of Europe, and more particularly in the southern and northern Netherlands, begins only in the second decade of the sixteenth century and is hardly mature before the 1560s. But the characteristic elaboration of the gables fronting the tall roofs of secular buildings occurred intermittently and recurrently from the first. Continuing in this respect the verticalism of Late Gothic architecture, Italianate proportions are usually ignored even where the apparatus of the Classical orders is employed on the surface of facades and their gables. Where, in the Renaissance architecture of the south, the orders establish the proportions, in the north they are usually no more than applied ornamentation, except when imported Italian designers and craftsmen were employed. That had already occurred in the 1530s in the case of Alessandro Pasqualini's IJsselstein tower near Utrecht in Holland and the Belvedere above Prague in Bohemia as begun by Paolo della Stella. On the Stadtresidenz in Landshut in Bavaria a whole team of Italians from Mantua also worked for years in the late 1530s and early 1540s.

It is rather the windows, so much larger and more closely spaced than in the south, that generally establish the basic ordonnance of northern facades: grids of small units separated by mullions in the southern Netherlands, larger openings subdivided by central members and by horizontal transoms in Holland. Crowning the regular fenestrated facades, and often as tall as the combined height of the storeys below, rise the gables. And the gables provide the principal, often the total, architectural interest of the facades by the concentration along their edges and on their plane surfaces of the architectural membering. In that membering orders and entablatures were only possible elements, not obligatory or even common ones. Included among the elements, increasingly from the late 1560s and more recurrent than pilasters and horizontal cornices or string-courses, is the sort of ornament usually called Northern Mannerist executed on so many gables at architectural scale. This ornament had been developed, if not in fact originated, in the southern Netherlands toward the midcentury and was soon being carried all over Europe by Antwerp publications (Figs. 38, 47, 48) of the 1550s and 1560s.

The present account, instead of discussing Netherlandish facades in their entirety, is therefore mostly concerned with gables. These were the dominant features in secular design through the later sixteenth century and well into the seventeenth. The most idiosyncratic elements in northern gable design were the relatively large scrolls that provided broken—one can almost say scalloped—outlines against the sky. But other equally common characteristics deserve particular mention at this point. In the detailed descriptions of scrolled gables that follow these characteristics are often taken for granted.

The usual building material of the Netherlandish Renaissance is exposed brick—also common in this period in southeastern England—not, as in German lands in the sixteenth century, stone or stuccoed brick. Long employed for the great medieval churches of such Baltic ports as Bremen, Lübeck, Wismar, and, far to the east, Gdańsk, brick contined in use not only as a vernacular building material but also for structures that were, at least relatively, quite monumental. Even in the southern Netherlands, where stone could more easily be transported down the rivers from the south and east, this is occasionally true. Moreover, a superior building material, the black marble often exported eastward for use in screens and tombs, came from Tournai in what is now southern Belgium and found especial favor both in the northern and the southern Netherlands.

The earlier portions of the *Palais de Savoie* (Savoy palace) at Mechelen (Malines) in Brabant of the first decade of the sixteenth century (Fig. 8) are of brick, though churches and public buildings in the Netherlands were likely to be of stone, at least in the south. All the same, at the Sint Janskerk, now the Catholic cathedral of 'sHertogenbosch in the northern Netherlands, the nave was completed in stone, in continuation of the earlier choir, in the first quarter of the sixteenth century. Sint Katerine at Hoogstraten, on the other hand, north of Antwerp but in Belgium today, was built in the second quarter of the century of brick by the architect Rombout Keldermans who worked elsewhere in stone, not only in Brabant and Flanders (Fig. 6), but also in Zeeland north of the Schelde. If stone was imported only for use on more representational structures as the over-all building material of facades, brick walls were yet likely to be liberally laced with the choicer material since that could be shaped by stonemasons and even carved by sculptors. Brick was not so often used quite alone except in vernacular building. Detailing in glazed or molded elements of baked clay, such as was rather common in earlier periods in the north particularly in cities on the Baltic such as Lübeck, had gone out of fashion in the Netherlands, if not to the north and east.

Stone-trimmed brick architecture is particularly omnipresent in what is today Holland. The stone-built town hall of Leiden (Fig. 79), for which the material was imported from Germany, is the most conspicuous exception and one dating from the 1590s long before the so much grander Raadhuis in Amsterdam was begun in 1648. But brick with stone trimming is equally characteristic of Denmark to the north, and all the way to northern Poland to the east. It is, indeed, the materials and their combination as much as the designs provided by Netherlanders which make such prominent monuments as the *Zielona Brama* (green gate) of the 1560s in Gdańsk (Fig. 54) and the Frederiksborg Slot at Hillerød in Denmark (Fig. 90) of forty years or so later look so Dutch.

The vigorously contrasted materials provide bichromatic surfaces of red broken by light-colored banding, not those minimal variations from monochromy usual by this date in most of Italy. Italians of the Renaissance, early and late, largely eschewed the bold banding of their Gothic ancestors in the *dugento* and the *trecento*. Instead, they commonly combined an architectural ordonnance of which the elements were executed in cut stone with neutral walling of tawny or dusty-colored brickwork. This marked difference seems to express what is almost as much a social as a geographical dichotomy. The characteristic choice of what was, after all, in much of the north the cheapest and most available material is as responsible for the particular look of Netherlandish Renaissance facades, both at home and abroad, as the middle-class status of the clients, whether corporate or individual. Yet representative public structures in the Low Countries were often all of stone, as in the case of the major town halls just mentioned, thus reflecting up to a point one of the princely characteristics of various direct Italian importations in the north. On the other hand, the building projects of such a prince as Christian IV of Denmark, all carried out in brick and mostly by Netherlanders, may well seem rather bourgeois in contrast to the Brussels palace of the French-born Cardinal Granvella. That must have been quite princely in its High Renaissance design to judge from Coetghebuer's early-nineteenth-century plates,[14] even though it was designed, like Christian's extensive works for the most part, by a Netherlander, in this case, Sebastiaan van Noyen.

A generation before Christian, Frederik II had commissioned his architect, Anthonis van Opbergen, who came from Mechelen in Brabant, to face the Kronborg Slot at Helsingør (Fig. 63) with stone, though otherwise the work is typically Netherlandish. In Christian's own generation, one can contrast his rather bourgeois taste, however luxurious its expression at Frederiksborg, the Rosenborg Slot in Copenhagen, and the Copenhagen Exchange (Figs. 90, 107–108), with the severe but distinctly princely artistic preferences of his sister Anne, the queen of James I of England and the patroness of Inigo Jones, as well as the more extravagant ones of his royal nephew, Charles I. What Christian built is much closer to such a private commission of the period in Denmark as the Sten Hus in Aalborg of the burgher Jens Bang (Fig. 109) than to the Queen's House at Greenwich or the Banquetting House in London, not to speak of Charles's project for a new palace in Whitehall.

But the choice and combination of materials is only one aspect, if an especially crucial one, of the taste that found architectural expression in the Netherlandish Renaissance from the 1560s well through the earlier decades of the next century. The initiatory works a hundred years before depended on the princely patronage of Margaret of Austria both at her Palais de Savoie in Mechelen (Figs. 11, 12) and at the *Vrij* in Brugge (Fig. 13); then came the work of imported Italians commissioned by Dutch lords in the 1530s at Breda, at IJsselstein and at Buren (Figs. 20, 21, 29) in the northern Netherlands, and later, in the 1550s, for Duke Wilhelm (or Willem) of Cleves, Berg, and Jülich, a magnate as much Dutch as German, at Jülich in the Rhineland. With such works, in this decade, the facade of *De Fonteine* in Gent in Flanders (Fig. 26), which is not at all princely, may be relevantly contrasted, for that will be more typical of Netherlandish design from this time on.

Despite the intrinsic interest and historical importance of such things as the IJsselstein tower and the Jülich *Zitadelle* as evidence of the gradual northern acceptance of Italian Renaissance discipline in the second quarter of the century, it is only with the next stylistic cycle that the main story in the Netherlands really takes shape in the 1550s and 1560s. This follows along the line announced by scroll-gabled facades, such as that of *De Fonteine*, which were erected for Dutch and Flemish burghers in the two preceding decades (Figs. 24, 43, 36). On the other hand, the monumental stone-built Raadhuis designed by Cornelis Floris for Antwerp, as begun in 1561 (Figs. 45, 46), must be considered truly princely, even though it was the middle-class *Raad* (city council) which was the corporate client. In any case, it was always exceptional in size and grandeur. More relevant, therefore, are much less grand edifices such as the house called *Het Meuleken* of 1552, which no longer survives, and the *Wenemaerhospital* of 1564 (Fig. 49), both in Gent, and *Huis Bethlehem* (Fig. 50) at Gorinchem (Gorkum) of 1566 in today's Dutch province of Zuid Holland. From the following 1570s and 1580s a good many more still stand in the north. These are chiefly in rather small places that have been little rebuilt since the seventeenth century. But old views of larger Dutch cities such as Amsterdam (Fig. 1) and the extensive ranges of guildhalls in the *Groote Markt* in Antwerp—much earlier in style on the one hand and much, much later in the date of their postwar reconstruction on the other (Fig. 66)—fill in the picture. Of these last, only the *Wewershuis*, the Drapers' Guildhall (Fig. 24), of the early 1540s, and the Sint Joris, or Archers' Guildhouse (Fig. 66), of around 1580 are still largely in original condition today, the one on the south side, the other on the north.

It is Arras in northern France, however, as already illustrated (Figs. 2, 3), for all the late-seventeenth- and eighteenth-century date of most of the house-fronts there, that gives the best idea of how many scroll-gabled facades there must once have been in Dutch towns, and doubtless in some of those of the southern Netherlands also. From the 1590s, moreover, through the earliest decades of the new century and well beyond, the numbers of scroll-gabled facades still in existence in Holland mount, reflecting the ever rising prosperity of the northern Netherlands in that period; fewer late examples seem to survive in such cities of the south as Antwerp, Gent, and Brugge; perhaps there never were so many.

Just after 1600 came the most extravagant example of all, the Great Arsenal (Figs. 91, 92), which is not in the Low Countries but at Gdańsk on the Baltic. This was erected by the Netherlander Anthonis van Opbergen, earlier Frederik II's architect in Denmark. He was commissioned not by the Swedish-born Polish king, Zygmunt III—whose up-to-date princely taste can best be appreciated in the suites of rooms he had imported Italian crafts-men redecorate for him in these same years in the Wawel in Kraków—but by the burghers of the city council, themselves mostly not Poles, but Germans, Netherlanders, and even Scotsmen.

In this period, and more particularly as the seventeenth century advanced, it was not German lands, much less Scotland, that produced the great painters of northern Europe, rivals in contemporary and later estimation of the southerners then active in Italy, in France, in Spain, and also in the north. Netherlandish painting is so much better known and ad-mired than Netherlandish architecture of the Renaissance that mention of a few painters may serve to relate, however loosely, the unfamiliar with the familiar, even if the genius of the greatest Dutch painters can hardly be compared with the admittedly lower level of artistic achievement of even the most talented architect-builders of this period in the north such as Opbergen.

The Biblical architecture of Rembrandt, mysterious and vaguely Oriental, certainly has nothing in common with the architectural production of the Netherlandish Renaissance except in being post-medieval, yet not at all characteristically either *cinquecento* or early Baroque. Almost as remote, but more comparable in providing direct evidence of the taste of Dutch burghers in the seventeenth century, are the chaste white-walled interiors, sparsely hung with maps and with mirrors, that were recurrently painted by Vermeer. But Vermeer does provide the finest view that survives, superior in quality to any topographical en-graving, of a seventeenth-century Dutch city in his *View of Delft* even though the town is seen from too great a distance to reveal much in detail about its architecture. There is, moreover, another painting of his that offers a detailed representation, as accurate undoubt-edly as any visual document could be, of a vernacular exterior, a subject in whose depiction Pieter de Hoogh characteristically joined him.

It is in the work of Frans Hals that a spirit more parallel to that of the architect-builders is recognizable. The lighthearted and slightly vulgar ostentation of the figures in Hals's group portraits, the very clarity and boldness of the coloring—if hardly bichromatic like the architecture—has something of the bourgeois assurance of the Dutch facades of his day, and particularly of the scrolled gables. The same is not so true of Rubens, for he represents a princely rather than a middle-class taste however nouveau riche. Moreover, his own house in Antwerp, thanks to his long stay in Italy, may more properly be defined as Italian Mannerist, indeed perhaps as proto-Baroque, rather than considered to be representative of the Netherlandish Renaissance, even at its end in the early seventeenth century.

On the other hand, the work of a different group of Dutch and, as they are often called, Flemish painters—artists such as Ostade, Teniers, or Brouwer—is often more similar to the flavor, if not to the actual ambience, of the work of the architects and the taste of the burghers who were their clients. That flavor is not quite the same, however, because the social tone of the painters' subjects—*ces magots*, as such a prince as Louis XIV later called them—is generally too low. The architecture is much closer in social tone to that of a less inelegant painter like Jan Steen: jolly, that is, rather than rowdy, though not so genteel and dainty as the work of "little masters" like Metsu or Terborch. Steen, incidentally, was a Catholic as was probably Vermeer—which is, in the present context, somewhat ironic.

Such superficial comparisons between contemporary phases of different arts are usually of no more than suggestive value even when, as with Vredeman, Sustris, or Rubens, painters were on occasion directly involved with architecture, or at least with large-scale decorative projects. Jan Vredeman de Fries hardly ranks as a painter with Rubens or even Sustris, but he is of major importance for his influence on architecture. With his name, however, should be paired that of the less published but more internationally employed and still highly esteemed sculptor Cornelis Floris. Their names bring up an idiosyncratic aspect of Netherlandish and, even more broadly, all Northern Renaissance architecture: that is the ornamental, a field of art in which Vredeman, if not Floris, made a greater contribution than in figural work. Ornament such as they developed is of more consequence than usual, particularly as regards the scrolled gables, once these artists' designs were in general circulation through engraved publications. These models for Northern Mannerist ornament (Figs. 34, 35, 38, 47) were issued, appropriately for the 1550s to the 1570s, in Antwerp; Vredeman, however, was Dutch, born at Leeuwarden in Friesland, as "de Fries" in his name indicates, though long settled in Antwerp. Vredeman published actual designs for scrolled gables (Fig. 48), as already mentioned. His ornament, however, as borrowed by others for use on innumerable gables, plays a broader role almost as conspicuously as do the flanking scrolls. These were first introduced long before, but achieved their richest and boldest forms as the boundaries of the crowning architectural display-pieces atop facades. Moreover, the particular Northern Mannerist elements of gable design continued in use from the 1560s onward for some two generations. By then, however, Vredeman's influence in the field of ornament had been partially superseded internationally by that of the German Wendel Dietterlin of Strasbourg, whose published work *Architectura* appeared in the late 1590s in Germany and in Alsace.

The climax of Northern Mannerism in architecture, as represented in the early decades by such major works of the seventeenth century outside the Netherlands as the arsenal in Gdańsk (Figs. 91, 92), the Frederiksborg Slot (Fig. 90) in Denmark, and the Stadtkirche at

Bückeburg in Germany, coincides rather closely in date with a reaction which may be loosely called Academic against that long-dominant style or mode. The most famous early examples exemplifying this reaction are the town halls in Augsburg and Nürnberg in Germany and the Queen's House and the Banquetting House in England, all designed and begun in the second decade of the century. But what was coming had been signaled a good deal earlier in the Netherlands by the *Bollaertskamer* in Gent (Figs. 70, 71) of the early 1580s in the south and by the *Waag* in Haarlem of the 1590s (Fig. 82) in the north. This is not to say, however, that the reaction spread over northern Europe from the Netherlands; Danes and Danzigers did not soon accept it, and its canonical models were not northern but Italian works of the period between the Council of Trent and the initiation of the Baroque. Some see this new anti-Mannerist or Academic phase as a belated triumph of the south over the north. Certainly its earliest sources in Italy are those of which reflections were brought north by southerners in the first decades of the sixteenth century and that northerners soon emulated at Augsburg and Mechelen. By this later time, however, around and after 1600, borrowings from the *quattrocento* had finally in northern Europe become quite out of date. As knowledge of more proximate *cinquecento* sources in standard Italian architecture of the mid- and late-sixteenth century reached the north through the illustrations in the books of Serlio, Vignola, and—most particularly for England—Palladio and Scamozzi, the influence of earlier models ended before long all over Europe except in the most backward rural areas and in the New World beyond the Atlantic.

The story thus came nearly full circle in a sort of century-long cultural spiral. Aspects of the earlier Italian invasion were paralleled—at least as regards the dependence of north-erners on southern sources—now that relevant models became available for imitation in illustrated treatises as they had never been earlier. More consequentially, moreover, the way was being prepared for the following wave of influence from Italy, that of the Baroque, toward which Maderno took an initial step in his Roman facade on S. Susanna of 1598–1603 in these same years.

Rather than conclude this Introduction by looking forward, however superficially, to the later acceptance of the mature Baroque in the north—more evident in German lands, in any case, than in Holland or the other countries with which this book is chiefly concerned—it is appropriate to turn well back to the very beginnings of the Renaissance and the origin of the scroll motif, originally a vertical volute, which was destined to be the most recurrent decorative element of the Netherlandish gable in the sixteenth and early seventeenth centuries, with additional comment on an alternative sort of Early Renaissance gable much used in northern Europe.

II The Scroll Motif in Italy and the North

SCROLLS AS VOLUTES; GABLES AS LUNETTES

AMONG the standard ingredients of Renaissance and later architectural design neither balustrades nor vertical scrolled elements were borrowed from antiquity. The first use of up-standing volutes was by Brunelleschi on the lantern of the Duomo in Florence. To quote Ludwig Heydenreich:[15] "round an octagonal columned tempietto . . . he set a ring of lower buttresses terminating in volutes. . . . The volute consists in an inspired reversal of the classical console. . . . From the lantern of Florence Cathedral the volute set out on its triumphal way. . . . The next example of their variation is Alberti's volutes on the facade of Santa Maria Novella," also in Florence but a good deal later.

The scale of the latter is much greater than that of Brunelleschi's volutes. Moreover, their location above the aisles flanking the pilastered and pedimented front of the clerestorey of the church provided a readily adaptable *parti* for total or partial facade-design employed for several centuries. Early examples are the facade of S. Francesco in Ferrara by Biagio Rossetti, dated 1494, and that of 1491–98 on Turin Cathedral by Meo da Caprino.[16] Somewhat later—c. 1515 according to Heydenreich—is the one in the perspective of a church by Leonardo da Vinci preserved at the Accademia in Venice.[17] This was the most paradigmatic of the early designs in its proportions and, indeed, was eventually repeated almost verbatim by the younger Antonio da San Gallo on S. Spirito in Sassia in Rome as built between 1537 and 1545.[18]

By that time scrolled gables—gables with flanking volutes—were no novelty in northern Europe. Except usually in England, roofs remained tall and steep-gabled; moreover, they were often broken by gabled dormers of brick or stone in the plane of the side facade. It will soon be evident that the North-European story was under way before the scroll-flanked facade had received what might be called "classic" expression in *cinquecento* Italy at the hands of San Gallo or been illustrated in a woodcut by Sebastiano Serlio. The first northern scrolled gable that can loosely be called Serlian was the one in the court of the Kasteel at Buren in Dutch Gelderland (Fig. 29) by Alessandro Pasqualini who, like Serlio, came from Bologna. That looked, at least, as if it were derived from the published design of Serlio for a *scena tragica* (Fig. 30) in his *Segundo libro*, published in Paris in 1545, and it must have dated from within the years while San Gallo's facade of S. Spirito was in construction in Rome. The two church facades Serlio illustrated in his *Quinto libro*, Paris, 1547, in Chap. 14 on folios 13 and 15, are closer to that of S. Spirito, but they appeared too late to influence early scrolled gables in the north as that of 1545 may have done, despite the very tight dating.

In one form or another, decorated gables without scrolling had long been the principal elements of architectural display in the Late Gothic secular architecture of northern Europe. Furthermore, the new scrolled gables were by no means just a peculiarity of the Netherlands. Builder-architects of Netherlandish origin eventually carried the motif both north into Denmark and far east along the Baltic coast, while in Germany a parallel sixteenth-century development of such features matched the contemporary flowering of the scrolled gable in what are today Holland and Belgium. A few words, therefore, should be said about what was happening as regards gable design in central Europe around 1520, when this story had its beginning. Morphologically, at least, the first Renaissance gables in Germany precede any in the Netherlands. Relatively simple, these are dependent on Italian sources little later in date than 1500. Thus they may still be considered, at least at second hand, as *quattrocento*. The term is not so applicable to what are presumably the oldest Netherlandish examples, but the latter cannot be described as *cinquecento* either.

A new, vaguely Renaissance, sort of gable certainly appeared early in the 1520s in Germany. Leonardo also seems to have projected one for the chateau of Romorantin in France before his death in 1519; but that is irrelevant here as it would hardly have been known in the north. The German gables have no scrolling but are just semicircular lunettes. They were added over all four sides of the *Dom* (cathedral) at Halle-a.-d.-Saale (Fig. 5) in Saxony, and it has been plausibly assumed that this was their first use. The Halle Dom was completed in the middle years of the 1520s[19] for Albrecht Cardinal Brandenburg, the Hohen-zollern prince who was both bishop of Magdeburg nearby and elector-archbishop of Mainz on the Rhine. Almost as soon, the motif was introduced in Westphalia on the Schloss at Schloss Neuhaus near Paderborn.[20] This Schloss Jörg Unkair rebuilt in the 1520s for Erich of Brunswick, who was the prince-bishop of Paderborn and, like Albrecht at Halle, the ruler of the region. Lunette gables, known in the vernacular as *welsche Gebel*—not, as in High German, *Giebel* (i.e., Italian gables)—continued to be built for decades, even in some places down to 1600 and beyond, although from the 1530s scrolled gables more and more supplanted them.[21]

However, the oldest surviving gables of scrolled outline are not in Germany but in certain port cities of the Netherlands: Mechelen[22] in Brabant and Brugge in Flanders. Once there were also Dutch examples of the 1530s and 1540s at Buren in Gelderland and in Utrecht that will shortly be described and illustrated (Figs. 29, 31). To judge from extant monuments in the southern Netherlands and from visual records of lost works in the north, the development of the scrolled gable—except at Mechelen—got under way in the Netherlands only in the 1530s, some ten years later than the *welsche Gebel* in Germany. Indeed, stepped gables continued in common use, both in the north and in the south, well into the seventeenth century, as also in Dutch Nieuw Amsterdam across the Atlantic. The earliest scrolled gables are, and probably always were, those that crown the north and northwest facades of the Palais de Savoie in Mechelen as noted earlier. These date, as far as can be determined from extant documents, from a few years—perhaps nearly a decade—before the lunette gables in Halle and at Schloss Neuhaus.[23]

THE NORTH IN THE EARLY SIXTEENTH CENTURY

The later wings of the Palais de Savoie are of unique importance at the beginning of the development of the scrolled gable in northern Europe. Before describing them in detail, however, something should be said concerning the general architectural situation in the Netherlands in the opening decades of the century. More specifically, the patronage of Margaret of Austria,[24] for whom the Palais de Savoie was erected, ought also to be summarized, and the careers of the builder and of the designer who worked for her at Mechelen should at least be sketched to the limited extent that sparse records permit.

Church-building of this period in what today are Holland and Belgium continued in a characteristic, but rather less autochthonous, late medieval vein than that of the latest German hall-churches, especially the ones in Saxony and Bohemia. Netherlandish ecclesiastical construction of the early decades of the century rarely rivals in architectural interest

—though it often does in scale—the late *Sondergotik* (special Gothic)[25] of the time farther east. Moreover, despite the relatively modest dimensions of the contemporary royal foundations of the Tudors in England—King's College Chapel, Cambridge; St. George's Chapel, Windsor; and Henry VII's Chapel at Westminster Abbey[26]—what was then being built in the Netherlands does not compare with them in quality.

So also the mature Flamboyant in the France of Louis XII and Francis I is, not unjustly, far better known and more generally admired than the Late Gothic churches in the Netherlands of which the execution continued that late. The grandeur of the war-damaged church of St.-Vulfran at Abbéville, of which the nave—still inaccessible—and the west front were finished by 1539, should be recalled especially, as also the less impressive but considerably earlier choir of St.-Etienne at Beauvais. Above all, there are the transepts of Beauvais Cathedral, in building through most of the first half of the sixteenth century,[27] with their overpoweringly tall and rich facades. (Even Ruskin, it might be noted, was seduced against his stern principles by St.-Vulfran.) The fine mortuary church Margaret of Austria built and furnished at Brou, just outside Bourg-en-Bresse in Franche-Comté, which was begun in 1513 and completed in 1532, counts as Netherlandish, however, though Bourg is today in eastern France. Her work there will be briefly discussed below.

The Cathedral of 'sHertogenbosch north of the Schelde, originally intended to serve only as the local parish church, has a high nave dated 1501–22.[28] The whole church is something of an exception in Holland because of its great size and its masonry vaults. Another notable exception is the very tall and rich spire topping the left-hand tower of Antwerp Cathedral in the southern Netherlands on which construction began in 1502. That was completed around 1521 about the same time as the 'sHertogenbosch nave.[29]

Despite a few such conspicuous ecclesiastical monuments, secular work in Brabant, above and below the present border between Holland and Belgium, is generally more interesting. That associated with Rombout II Keldermans (1460–1531)[30] is especially relevant here since it was he whom Margaret of Austria employed, not in 1513 at Brou, but a few years later in Mechelen. On the Antwerp spire, however, Keldermans, son and brother of well-established architect-builders, did not work alone but in collaboration with his contemporary Domien de Waghemaekere. (Domien or Dominicus, 1460–1542, had been city architect of Antwerp since 1502 in succession to his father Herman.) Preceding that major commission south of the Schelde had come Rombout's considerably earlier association with the rebuilding by his father, Anthonis I Keldermans (d. 1512), over the years 1506–12 of the front of the Raadhuis at Middelburg. That large port town is on the Wester Schelde in the present-day Dutch province of Zeeland. The elaborate Late Gothic facade in Middelburg was eventually finished by Rombout toward 1520, a few years after he began to work for Margaret of Austria at Mechelen. In 1512, he had taken charge of the completion of the church at nearby Veere, bringing the tower to its present great height in 1521 about the time he was completing the Antwerp spire. In 1515 he succeeded his brother Anthonis II on the latter's death as city architect of Mechelen where they had both been born.

Keldermans's most important work, other than his addition to the Palais de Savoie, is the north wing of the Raadhuis of Gent in Flanders. On that he was engaged in association with Waghemaekere—as at first in Antwerp—from 1518 until his death in 1531.[31] With the Antwerp architect, who completed the Gent Raadhuis in 1535, Rombout collaborated not only in Gent and in Antwerp but also on the *Maison du Roi* (Broodhuis), the long-lost residence of the Habsburgs in Brussels, which had been begun by the elder Keldermans, Anthonis I, for Emperor Maximilian in 1514 or 1515.[32]

The Town Hall at Gent (Fig. 6) is the lushest extant example of Brabantine secular Late Gothic, more than rivaling even the Middelburg Raadhuis, though it ornaments a still-prosperous port that is not in Brabant but in Flanders. Gables were designed for it, as is known from surviving drawings (Fig. 7), and originally it had gabled dormers (Fig. 71) as well. Of the Maison du Roi, which Rombout and Waghemaekere eventually completed for Maximilian's grandson and successor, Charles V,[33] nothing survives in the existing building of 1875-85. This is "revived" Brabantine Late Gothic in style and faces the heavily restored fifteenth-century Hotel de Ville across the Grande Place in Brussels.

The St. Katerina-kerk at Hoogstraten north of Antwerp was begun in 1524,[34] just before work on the Palais de Savoie was probably coming to a conclusion, at the behest of the local count, Antoine de Lalaing. For that Rombout alone was responsible. A very large but plain church of brick in a small village, this was much damaged in the last war but has been completely restored. Rombout's rather retardataire Gothic here has little relation to the sumptuous secular work on which he was employed with others in Middelburg and Gent (Fig. 6). But the flowing patterns of the window tracery, within which the design of the glass, dated 1528-35, is already of Renaissance character, should be mentioned.

Finally, as late as 1529 or 1530 Rombout provided, shortly before his death, a Brabantine Late Gothic design (of which elevational drawings survive) for what is now the north wing of the Mechelen Raadhuis.[35] Intended by Charles V to house the *Groote Raad* (grand council) of the Netherlands, this was left an unfinished fragment when Brussels eventually replaced Mechelen as the regional seat of Habsburg rule. The wing at Mechelen was only completed, following rather closely on the long side the original drawing by Keldermans, in the years 1902-13. In quality it naturally resembles more the Maison du Roi as rebuilt in the late nineteenth century than it does the Gent Raadhuis.

In 1512, despite his recorded activity at that point north of the Schelde in Zeeland, Rombout is believed by some to have visited Italy. Such a hypothetical trip has, however, little or no relevance to the greater part of his production. Except for the northern wings of the Palais de Savoie, all of it remained consistently Late Gothic. Somewhat as in the slightly earlier case of Beneš Rejt (Benedikt Ried or von Launa)[36] in Bohemia, however, it was this latest Gothic architect of Brabant who first carried out Renaissance work at full architectural scale in the Netherlands when called on to extend Margaret's palace in Mechelen.

That commission was almost precisely contemporary with the gilded bronze *Epitaph* (wall monument) of Jakob von Croy, preserved in the Treasure of Cologne Cathedral, which was executed in the Netherlands.[37] Despite its miniature size, this is already a work of Renaissance design by a Netherlander that can be considered truly architectural, not a mere decorative accessory to a painting or a window. It has, however, no gable. More relevant here in any case are the larger works that were being carried out for Margaret of Austria at this time at Brou in Franche-Comté as well as at Mechelen in Brabant.

THE PATRONAGE OF MARGARET OF AUSTRIA

Maximilian had made his able daughter Margaret—by that time the widow of Duke Philibert of Savoy—stadholder of the Netherlands in 1507 after the death of her brother Philip the Fair the year before, though her young nephew Charles,[38] born at Gent in Flanders, then became titular ruler of the province since he was Philip's son. Margaret was, moreover, charged with Charles's education. As first built just after her arrival in Mechelen, presumably by Anthonis I and Anthonis II Keldermans, Rombout's father and brother, who were successively the local city architects, the palace is a rather simple though quite large Late Gothic domestic structure of stone-trimmed brick surrounding on three sides an internal court (Fig. 8). This court has ranges of four-centered arcading under the south wing and along that on the east; but there are few other architectural features except for the many stepped gables, the very ordinary stone-mullioned windows of rectangular shape, and the larger pointed and tracery-filled ones of the chapel (Fig. 9). The much more interesting north wing and northwest corner of the palace were begun in 1517 and probably carried to completion by 1526, still for Margaret. These dates are awkwardly loose as termini when it comes to relating her new work to such other very early examples of Renaissance architectural design exported from the Netherlands as the Croy tomb of 1518 and the Hackeney screen of the 1520s (Fig. 10), both in Cologne. The latter is usually presumed to be the work of Jan van Roome, one of the Netherlanders Margaret employed at Brou.

The contrast on the Palais de Savoie between the stepped gables of the earlier portions— the inherited medieval sort that would continue in general use in both the southern and the northern Netherlands through the century and into the next—and the scrolled gables of the later wings (Figs. 11, 12) emphasizes the innovative originality of the latter.

In 1516 Charles's Spanish grandfather Ferdinand died, three years before Maximilian. Possessed thenceforth of the latter's crown of Aragon—and effectively also of his grandmother Isabella's crown of Castile because of the recognized incapacity of his mother Joanna the Mad—Charles's interest in his native Netherlands diminished though it never ceased altogether. Charles was not, however, at any time a very active patron of architecture in the Low Countries; at least almost nothing he commissioned is now extant other than the structure that Keldermans began at Mechelen to house the Groote Raad, and even that was largely carried out, as has been noted, only in this present century. Charles's one other architectural project in the Netherlands of any consequence was the completion of the Maison du Roi in Brussels, of which the construction had already been underway for some five or six years when he became emperor in 1520.

Neither the Mechelen nor the Brussels building, both Brabantine Late Gothic in style, was at all like the grand High Renaissance palace Pedro Machuca (d. 1550) began for him at Granada in Spain in the late 1520s.[39] Charles, however, eventually undertook the construction of new fortifications in the north. In the early 1540s he brought to the Netherlands for this program the military engineer Donato de' Buoni (or Bono) Pellizuoli from Bergamo to take charge at Antwerp and elsewhere. This Italian, moreover, was responsible for the architectural design of the demolished Sint Joris (Mechelen) Gate at Antwerp in 1545, which he built in association with the Netherlander Sebastiaan van Noye or Noyen (?1493–1557).[40] But that is well ahead of the story as regards the earlier decades of the century.

Unlike her nephew, Margaret was an enthusiastic and even a rather ambitious builder. Already, by 1517 or not long after, she was evidently prepared to sponsor major architectural innovation on her Mechelen palace rather than continue the work as it had been begun some ten years before (Figs. 8, 9). But her patronage of architecture had its start elsewhere. After she had been widowed for the second time, her father made her regent of Franche-Comté. Just before settling in Mechelen, she began in 1506 to erect outside Bourg-en-Bresse, her principal seat in that province, conventual buildings at Brou. These were intended to serve the church she was planning as a memorial to her late husband Philibert of Savoy and his mother Marguerite de Bourbon. In fact, Marguerite de Bourbon had vowed much earlier to endow a new church at Brou.

When Maximilian made Margaret of Austria stadholder of the Netherlands the next year she left Franche-Comté and began to build at Mechelen in Brabant what was then called from her occupancy the Palais de Savoie. This is now the seat of the *Gerechtshof* (courts of justice) of the small Belgian city—and best so identified in Mechelen which is not French-speaking today. After Margaret's time, when Charles's sister Mary of Hungary was governing the Netherlands from Brussels as viceroy in the mid-sixteenth century, the palace housed his chancellor, Cardinal Granvella. Charles had made this Burgundian seigneur de Granvelle archbishop of the newly created see of Mechelen and Philip II, later, named him primate of the southern Netherlands as his successor today is of Belgium. From 1616 to 1794 the palace was occupied by the Groote Raad.

Margaret did not forget her plans for Brou.[41] That eventually became one of the most notable of all Late Gothic churches on the continent, rivaling as a monumental funerary edifice Henry VII's chapel at Westminster. In 1512, after considering the French sculptor Jean Perréal (c. 1455–1530), she commissioned a Netherlander to design the Brou church: Louis van Bodeghem (c. 1470–1540)[42] from Brussels. Bodeghem had been employed there on the Maison du Roi by her father Maximilian. Construction started in June 1513. Bodeghem then called in another Netherlander, Jean de Bruxelle (mentioned earlier as Jan van Roome),[43] to design the tombs of Philibert, of his mother, and of Margaret herself. At the time of Margaret's death in 1530 the carving of the choir stalls by local French rather than imported Netherlandish craftsmen had just started. That finally brought the church to completion two years later.

The three tombs at Brou were initiated in 1516 shortly before work started on the later wings of Margaret's palace in Mechelen. Like that, they were not finished for a decade and, indeed, considerably longer. The execution of the life-size *gisants*, commissioned from the German sculptor Conrat Meit (c. 1475–1550)[44] in 1526, the same year the wings at Mechelen were very likely finished, was completed only after Margaret's death.

All the Brou tombs are Brabantine Late Gothic in style, and so also is the elaborate retable in the Lady Chapel. These decorative extravaganzas of Jura alabaster and black Tournai marble were carried out in a manner fully worthy of Rombout Keldermans. Margaret might well have employed him to design them, since, as has been noted, he had in the previous year, 1515, become city architect of Mechelen in succession to his brother Antonis II. Only the *putti* on the tombs illustrate the new Italianism already so evident in the hybrid design of the somewhat later[45] Hackeney screen (Fig. 10) in Cologne. Like the *gisants*, these *putti* were probably carved by Meit, whose sculpture elsewhere has an increasingly Italianate flavor.

Originally from Worms, Meit had worked earlier at Wittenberg as a sculptor for the elector of Saxony, Luther's protector Friedrich der Weise, and then for Philip the Fair in Mechelen. It was almost a decade before the *gisants* in the Brou church were commissioned, however, that Margaret called, not on Bodeghem nor on Meit—whom she was, in fact, probably not yet employing—but more appropriately on Rombout Keldermans, the Mechelen city architect, to extend the Palais de Savoie, though she did not entrust the designing to him.

Margaret, despite her Habsburg father, can hardly be considered a German or Austrian patron of art any more than her nephew Charles; nor, except for Meit, who had in any case earlier worked for her brother in the Netherlands, did she employ Germans. Culturally, her background was Burgundian and even French. Her mother was Mary of Burgundy, and she had been brought up at the court of Louis XI of France. When very young, indeed, she had been nominally married to the dauphin, later Charles VIII. Savoy, moreover, was French rather than Italian in this period; and her latest husband's mother, as noted, was Marguerite de Bourbon. Influences from contemporary France might be expected in her enlarged mansion, even though at Brou in Franche-Comté she employed no French artists until her very last years.

THE NORTH WINGS OF THE PALAIS DE SAVOIE IN MECHELEN

In the work of the late teens and twenties that rounds out Margaret's ten-year-old palace in Mechelen, the arches of the new arcade on the court running across the north wing are mostly still four-centered like the Late Gothic ones on the court side of the earlier wings (Fig. 8). The entrance arch, however, is semi-elliptical. Thus it rather resembles the arches of the loggia, dating from late in the first decade of the century, which once had a conspicuous place on Cardinal Georges d'Amboise's chateau of Gaillon in Normandy.[46] Such arches can still be seen on the surviving portal of the chateau as reërected in the forecourt of the Ecole des Beaux-Arts in Paris.

The compound piers of this later arcade at the Palais de Savoie are square in plan, not polygonal like the earlier ones in the Mechelen court as begun in 1507, and faced with paneled pilasters. The panels are not, like the ones of a decade or so earlier at Gaillon that were executed by imported Italian craftsmen, decorated with carved arabesques in the *quattrocento* way, but quite plain. Except for the four-centered arches, however, none of the elements on Margaret's later wing is still as Late Gothic as the initiatory work at Gaillon of the opening years of the century before the imported Italians came on the job there in 1508; nor does anything, for that matter, suggest the hand of Rombout Keldermans personally—not at least as that can be recognized in his major works surviving from this period, the portion of the Gent Raadhuis initiated by him together with Waghemaekere in 1518 (Fig. 6) and the Hoogstraten church he began on his own in 1524. As has been indicated, moreover, he continued to his death to work elsewhere only in Brabantine Late Gothic. It must have been Margaret's own decision, not his, to erect a Renaissance addition to her still relatively new Late Gothic palace and to place a different designer, the mysterious Guyot de Beaugrant, in effective command, with Keldermans serving as "master of the work" but not as architect in our sense of that word.

But who was Beaugrant, where was he trained, and what were his models? Available information about him is scant and ambiguous, indeed only conjectural as to his origin or his training.[47] As a sculptor—if we are actually concerned with the same artist?—Guyot's principal surviving work, also commissioned by Margaret, is the chimneypiece and associated decoration in the *Vrij* at Brugge (Fig. 13) in Flanders. This elaborate sculptural program inside the Burg was carried out in 1529–30, chiefly in polished black Tournai marble and carved oak, to a design provided in 1528 by the painter Lancelot Blondeel (1496–1561).[48] It was intended by Margaret to celebrate the Treaty of Cambrai between Charles V and Francis I that she and the French king's mother, Louise de Bourbon, had negotiated —hence called the Ladies Peace. The Brugge decorations are in their architectural elements much less consistently Renaissance in character than the Mechelen palace (Figs. 11, 12), though by no means so residually Late Gothic as the building for the Groote Raad that Keldermans began at that later time. All the same they are evidence of a considerable change in Margaret's taste since she originally commissioned the tombs at Brou early in the previous decade.

Shortly before the work at the Vrij was undertaken, however, in 1526 when that on the Palais de Savoie was probably being concluded, Guyot de Beaugrant had executed at Brussels in St. Jacques-sur-Coudenberg the lost tomb[49] of Margaret's brother, the Archduke Francis, who had died when very young forty-five years earlier. That followed a more or less Renaissance design not of his own invention but provided by Louis van Bodeghem. Though the latter had been supervising the work at Brou since 1516, he had there employed, not Beaugrant, but Jan van Roome to design the three tombs and, at this later point, Meit for the figural sculpture.

Despite the major work at Brugge and the minor work in Brussels, Beaugrant seems to have continued to live in Mechelen after the completion of the Palais de Savoie. But in 1533 he went to Spain, presumably in the service of Charles V, settled in Bilbao, and died there in 1551. This later career offers no clues as to his origin and training, and only by implication of his contemporary reputation. If he was Burgundian, that is, Franc-comtois, one might expect to find him employed by Margaret at Brou before the later wings of the Palais de Savoie were begun. In the entry in Thieme-Becker, he is assumed to have been a Netherlander, but a Walloon, not a Fleming or from Brabant, and it is noted that this family name is found in the fifteenth century in the southern Netherlands. Von der Osten and Vey believe he came from Lorraine, however. Beaugrant's later employment, from the mid-1520s on, indicates that contemporaries considered him primarily a sculptor—as has also been true of modern scholars—and even one usually employed as executant rather than as designer. That seems more than a little confusing—unless, indeed, there were two Guyots with somewhat similar family names!

Turning to such inferences as can be drawn from the palace itself (Figs. 11, 12), one may say that—except perhaps for the balustraded balconettes and the recurrent low-pitched pediments—there is not much to suggest such firsthand knowledge of Italy as do the Fugger commissions at Augsburg in Germany of 1510-15 for the burial chapel at St. Anna and the houses in the Weinmarkt.[50] Other work there and at Regensburg designed by, or attributed to, Hans Hieber[51] also recalls a little Venetian architecture of around 1500 which the Fuggers—though less probably their executant artists—certainly knew well.

It is not plausible to assign essential responsibility for the design of the later wings of the Palais de Savoie to Rombout Keldermans, even on the strength of a possible visit to Italy five years earlier. Nor does any other work of his imply the relevant knowledge of *quattrocento* architecture that Beneš Rejt in Prague and Sebastian Loscher in Augsburg had somehow acquired well before this, much less the expertise of such imported Italians as Francesco Fiorentino and Bartolommeo Berrecci in Kraków[52] or Giovanni da Fiesole at Rennes and Girolamo Viscardi at St. Denis.[53]

In the loose organization of the exterior massing of the northern wings of the Palais de Savoie (Fig. 11) symmetry is confined to certain portions of the composition: the portal on the left; then the main north gable; next, the section of wall to the right; and, around the northwest corner, each of the two other gables (Fig. 12). Every portion is carefully organized within itself but never repeats its neighbors. For example, no one sort of scrolled gable is consistently used, but rather several variants. The whole has little resemblance, therefore, to the monotonous, if frequently broken, rhythms of Brabantine Late Gothic secular architecture (Fig. 4) or to the relative regularity, of a Venetian *quattrocento* kind, characteristic of the preceding and contemporary work in the German cities in the upper Danube valley.

The several tall gables of the Palais de Savoie and the concentration on them of most of the decoration have, to modern eyes, a distinctly Netherlandish air. Certainly the tall scrolled gables on the Palais de Savoie are not Italian in concept, despite their detailing, nor do they look French.[54] They are, rather, the most original features.

No conclusion need be drawn from the particular sort of massing of the later wings of the Palais de Savoie. Yet what Margaret built does recall more than a little such a great French town mansion of the previous century as the house of Jacques Coeur at Bourges.[55] The gabled stone dormers (Figs. 11, 12), moreover, have a distinctly François Ier air. This is especially true of the way they break across the crowning members of the wall on the outer side of the north wing and also on the west side of the court. The one on the north wing, indeed, is linked in a French manner by vertical strips to a window in the main storey below. With its flanking pilasters, small concave scrolls, and pedimental termination, the dormer on the exterior is somewhat similar to the nearly contemporary ones on the court side of Francis I's new wing at Blois, built over the years 1515-24, and even more to those on the late wing at Amboise (Fig. 14), which must be of about the same date.[56]

The much flattened elliptical arches on the main gable above the north front recall French examples, even earlier than those at Blois, on Georges d'Amboise's extant gatehouse at Gaillon (Fig. 15), which was begun in 1508 and completed by the time of his death in 1510.[57] Yet, except for these arches and, perhaps, the delicate scale of the applied orders, the detail is not as French in character as on some English tombs and so forth of much the same years.[58] Neither, however, is it Florentine or Venetian like that on various portals; tombs and, indeed, several whole chapels in Poland and Bohemia, in Austria and Hungary, and even in Germany that were in construction by the time—and, in several cases at least, a decade or more before—the work at Mechelen was completed.

The horizontal stratification of these crowning features above the eaves line of the north front of the Palais de Savoie, later common on Renaissance gables in the Netherlands both south and north, seem to reflect the separation of storeys by horizontal elements seen on many Late Gothic guildhalls and the like. In such design, Gothic string-courses are, in a sense, "translated" into cornices or whole entablatures. The framing of the windows at Mechelen by engaged columns resembles only very slightly, however, the molded vertical elements in relief that create, together with ranges of four-centered or semicircular arches, an all-over grid on various early-sixteenth-century facades surviving in Gent (Figs. 18, 19) and elsewhere in Flanders and Brabant.

There is, indeed, no suggestion of such a grid in the treatment of the walls of the later wings of the Palais de Savoie (Fig. 11). The particular proportions and the wide spacing of the large windows actually follow Italian rather than northern precedent more closely than do most other elements of the facades. Various Italians, mostly such men as Pietro Torrigiani[59] from Florence and Jacopo de' Barbari from Venice[60] who are not usually associated with the design of buildings, were early visitors at Margaret's court. Some may have lingered in Mechelen long enough into these years to advise on the Palais de Savoie. The most likely might have been the painter Tommaso Vincidor from Bologna. He worked a little later on the Kasteel at Breda in Holland[61] and even introduced there some decorated gables and gablets (Figs. 22, 23), though these do not much resemble the ones at Mechelen. However, Vincidor was sent north by Leo X only in 1520, after the construction of these wings was almost certainly under way and the major design decisions already made.

The boldest and, for German lands as well as for the work of Netherlanders at home and abroad, the most premonitory elements here are the big scrolls that enliven the silhouette of the larger gables against the sky (Figs. 11, 12). The S-curved ones flanking the second stage above the main line of the eaves seem almost proto-Baroque in their exuberance, if not the plainer ones on the next stage just below the simple segmental pediment that crowns the whole. That pediment is not very like, however, the semicircular lunette gables known as *welsche Gebel* that would make their first appearance in Germany on the Dom at Halle

(Fig. 5) and at Schloss Neuhaus near Paderborn by the mid-1520s, just the years when the Palais de Savoie was probably being brought to completion. Moreover, at the top of one gable around the corner on the northwest a steep-pointed pediment, with sides which follow the slope of the roof, replaces the segmental sort (Fig. 12). To be noted also are the urns, and more especially the balls, punctuating the outlines of the gables much as on innumerable later ones, especially in Germany, dating from the mid-1520s to well after 1600.

None of this repertory bears a close resemblance to the Italianate detail of the northern painters Margaret favored, neither to the profusion of their still *quattrocento* arabesque ornament, nor to the rather High Renaissance orders they occasionally introduced as framing elements or in backgrounds.

In considerable part the hard metallic quality of the surfaces of most of the cut-stone trim on the Palais de Savoie is doubtless the result of nineteenth-century restoration. Thus also, some of the features discussed above may have been modified by the architect in charge of that, L. Blomme, in 1878. Yet such apparently anachronistic features as the proto-Baroque scrolls were all but matched in Germany already in the mid-1530s by those on the gables of the north wing of the Schloss at Neuburg-a.-d.-Donau in the Upper Palatinate (Fig. 16). Other things, such as the balconettes and, more especially, the large rectangular doorways leading to them, seem somewhat uncoordinated with the rest of the facade. These might, perhaps, have been introduced later in the sixteenth century[62] (Fig. 11). In this connection Cardinal Granvella's occupancy of the Palais de Savoie in the mid-century, while van Noyen was building for him the new palace in Brussels, mentioned earlier, in what would seem to have been an advanced—one might almost say High Renaissance or even Academic—style, is perhaps relevant.

The portal at the left of the north facade of the Palais de Savoie (Fig. 17), the dominant feature of its own symmetrical composition, deserves further comment. The entrance arch, which is half-round, not flattened, is framed by pairs of ungrammatically slim colonnettes set on podia. Above, there is a more conventionally proportioned entablature broken by *ressauts* over the pairs of colonnettes; between the entablature and the top of the wall a shallow niche shelters a modern carving of the arms of Mechelen. The flat lintel over this curves down at either end, providing a broader version of the flattened arches on the main north gable. The motif can be matched on the Gaillon portal, dating from before 1508, now set up in the court of the Ecole des Beaux-Arts in Paris.

Breaking forward from the low roof over the portal of the Palais de Savoie is a highly decorated gable. The treatment of the gable is edicular, with a tall central niche in which there is a modern (?) allegorical statue; but this stage is broadened at the base by S-scrolls to form a feature remarkably like the one over the Porta della Rana on the Cathedral of Como, executed about 1490 by the Rodaris.[63] A little later, in the mid-1530s that may have influenced the Georgenbau portal of the Residenzschloss at Dresden;[64] but knowledge of such an Italian model, though possible, is not likely at Mechelen so early. The crowning elements are less similar to those on later Renaissance gables in northern Europe, however, than the treatment of the larger ones to the right and around the corner on the west (Figs. 11, 12). On the other hand, the gable over the entrance approaches more closely in its elaboration the dormers above the facades of Francis I's wings at Blois and Amboise (Fig. 14) than do the plainer dormers here on the Palais de Savoie that were described earlier.

Thus several, at least, of the motifs used on the entrance to the Palais de Savoie support the conclusion that Beaugrant's inspiration came from France, not directly from Italy as actual emulation of the Porta della Rana would imply. The fact that Margaret's later wings on the palace, begun in 1517, were all but precisely contemporary with the wings at Blois of 1515–24 and the one at Amboise[65] need not make unlikely generic—if not necessarily specific—influence from French work of the period. It should be recalled that the gatehouse at Gaillon (Fig. 15) was begun almost a decade prior to the years in which the construction of these wings got under way, and the main chateau there largely before that, earlier in the first decade of the century. Several of the chimneypieces in the interior at Mechelen support this conclusion. Yet these seem to have been "renewed" in the nineteenth century and may even be largely of Blomme's design. That could discount their relevance to the question of French influence in Margaret's time since he would naturally have leaned on authentic French models of the sixteenth century.

It is curious that this remarkable monument, rivaling in interest and in historical importance even Gaillon and the chateaux of the Loire, should have been almost totally without influence either in its own region or abroad in the 1520s, to judge at least from what has survived. A notable exception is the gable of 1526 or 27 on the *Metselaershuis*[66] (*De Engel der Metsers*) at Gent in Flanders. This facade, as rebuilt now facing on the Graslei, is Gothic as a whole (Fig. 18), but it has large near-circular C-scrolls at the sides which seem to parody those on the Palais de Savoie. The nearby *Vrijeschippershuis* of 1530–31 (Fig. 19), also on the Graslei, has no such scrolls, though the big S-curved elements on that—if hardly Renaissance in character—are nonetheless even more inappropriate in their vigorous horizontality to the otherwise standard Late Gothic design than the scrolls on the earlier facade.[67]

III   Italians in Holland

BY THE 1530s literate design of Renaissance inspiration was beginning to appear in Holland. This was thanks to the occasional employment of Italians, just as had already been true long before this far to the east in Hungary and in Poland, though not so early in England, much less the German lands in the center of Europe. Just as the stylistic innovations at the Palais de Savoie in the south are associated with work commissioned by Charles V's representative, his aunt Margaret, in the north the patron was Charles's deputy, Hendrick (III) of Nassau-Breda, who was stadholder in the northern Netherlands. Like Margaret, Hendrick was an enthusiastic builder. Work on the principal church in Breda, O. l. Vrouwenkerk, particularly the choir and associated chapels, went on into the 1540s but remained wholly Gothic in style. On the other hand, several tombs which must date from the 1530s, that of one of Hendrick's predecessors as stadholder, Engelbert II of Nassau (d. 1504) and his wife Cimburga van Baden (d. 1501), and that of Frederik van Renesse (d. 1538) and his wife, Anna van Hamale van Elderen, who survived him, are of Renaissance design.[68] Neither for the Engelbert monument, which is wholly sculptural, nor the Renesse tomb, which occupies an Italianate niche, are the designers or the executants known; but certainly the sculptor of the Engelbert tomb was a foreigner, though probably not one of the two Italians Hendrick was then employing on the Breda Kasteel, for neither of them was a sculptor.

It is in work done at the Kasteel of Breda, now the Koniglijk Militaire Akademie, how-

29

ever, that gables relevant to this account appeared, first on the outer works as erected for Hendrick over the years following 1532, and then on the main quadrangular structure of 1536–38.[69] Of the earlier work little is extant except for the portal. That seems surprisingly "correct" for its date, in part because of remodeling in the eighteenth century. The original pediment over the entrance, supported by the well-proportioned compound order that survives, was still sharply pointed like a gable, as can be seen in early views (Fig. 20); the open gallery that once existed above was curiously roofed with a range of tiny cross-gables decorated with scrolling dolphins. The portal and the gablets are the work of Alessandro Pasqualini (1485–1559), who was building in the same years the more remarkable Bramantesque tower of the church at IJsselstein, a village near Utrecht.

Pasqualini came from Bologna and was employed at first, like so many Italians working abroad in the mid-sixteenth century—when siege warfare was rapidly changing because of the use of artillery—as a military engineer to advise on fortifications, in his case those of Amsterdam, 'sHertogenbosch, and Middelburg, all in the northern Netherlands. That explains the particular location of his work at the Kasteel in Breda.

At IJsselstein, Pasqualini had a different client. Most probably this was the Count of Buren, Floris van Egmond,[70] who is recorded as employing him in the 1530s and early 1540s on the no longer extant castle at Buren. Though it is known today only from an eighteenth-century drawing, Pasqualini provided there a central projection on the court facade of the main block and capped it with what must have been the earliest example of a scrolled gable in Holland (Fig. 29). A description of that will shortly follow.

At Breda, Pasqualini was succeeded by another Bolognese, Tommaso di Andrea Vincidor, who was mentioned earlier. He was responsible for the design of the main quadrangular structure of the Kasteel. That was begun in 1536, the year of Vincidor's death, though not completed until well into the seventeenth century because of Hendrick's death in 1538. As earlier noted, Vincidor, a painter, had come north from Rome in 1520 when Leo X sent him to supervise the weaving of the Raphael tapestries for the Sistine Chapel. By the mid-1530s he had been in the north, chiefly in Antwerp and in Mechelen, long enough to be influenced by northern ideas of architectural design somewhat as Sebastiano Serlio would be in France in the next decade. Yet the relative "correctness"[71] of the Kasteel by sixteenth-century Italian standards is somewhat unexpected considering how drastically the Italian Boccador's design for Chambord in France was modified in execution not so long before. That resulted from the employment of local builders such as, presumably, Vincidor had to work with here. All the same he, or whoever carried on after his death, topped the court facades (Fig. 21) with tiny scrolled gables very similar to those over Pasqualini's outworks and larger decorated gables were introduced above the entrance and at the southwest corner (Figs. 22, 23).

These larger gables on the Breda Kasteel hardly look like the work of an Italian, yet they do not appear either to have been a development or a modulation from the ones of the previous decade at Mechelen (Figs. 11, 12). They are staged, like those on the Palais de Savoie, but there are no large scrolled elements on the sides of the second stage (Fig. 22). Instead, the transition from the three-bay width of the wing below at the southwest corner to the one-bay width of the middle stage is effected by sculptural elements, curious dragon-like creatures combined with small scrolls.[72] The other gable in the center of the main front was similarly decorated though it did not top a projection (Fig. 23). Reflections of these would appear a few years later on Johan van Rossum's long-lost house at Zaltbommel (Fig. 32). Above his brother Maerten's surviving gatehouse there of the mid-1530s, however, the gables are all of the old stepped pattern. On the other hand, the dormers on the exterior at Breda, with sharp-pointed gablets ornamented by scrolling dolphins (Fig. 23), were repeated in the next decade on the so-called *Duivelshuis* built for Maerten at Arnhem (Fig. 28).

IV Dutch and German Gables
1530–50

GABLES OF THE 1530S IN GERMANY AND THE
SOUTHERN NETHERLANDS

AMONG WORKS of the 1530s in the southern Netherlands nothing survives that is much like the Breda Kasteel, much less the church tower at IJsselstein, in the north. All the same it is in Antwerp, the chief commercial and financial center of the Western world in this period, or in Brussels, from the midcentury decades the seat of the viceroy Mary of Hungary, that one might expect to find facades of Charles's time capped with decorated gables reflecting or paralleling those at Mechelen. Around 1550, as was noted earlier, Charles's principal minister, Cardinal Granvella, had Sebastiaan van Noyen erect for him a palatial High Renaissance mansion in Brussels with no gables of any sort as far as is known. Neither that nor any earlier Italianate work is extant there, however, because of the great fire of 1695—if, indeed, such ever existed other than Granvella's palace. As regards gables, none elsewhere in the south surviving from these years parallels those at Breda; rather, the stepped gables used on the earlier portion of the Palais de Savoie were still favored through much of the rest of the century. Such a gable exists, for example, on the *Waterhuys*, now Museum Brouwershuis, begun in 1553[73] in Antwerp. That fortunately stands well outside the Groote Markt in the Adriaan Brouwersstraat and was therefore spared in the holocaust of 1576.

The fire set by the Spanish in 1576 in the Antwerp Groote Markt was not so destructive as that in the Grande Place of Brussels a century later. But the gabled facades of the guild-houses on the north side—some Late Gothic, others much more advanced in design and of seventeenth-century date originally—were all rebuilt or restored after that disaster, again after World War I, and once more after the damage done in World War II. Thus, whatever their present appearance, very few really belong to this period. None older than the *Wewershuis* (drapers' guildhouse),[74] known formerly as *D' Oude Waghe* or *De Gulde Balance*, at No. 38 on the south side (Fig. 24) which is of the early 1540s has any post-Gothic elements.

At Charles's behest, Rombout Keldermans began the building, not in Antwerp, but at Mechelen, intended to house the Groote Raad, now part of the Raadhuis, in a Late Gothic mode as late as 1529 or 1530 as already noted; but the gable dates from 1902–13. The still more elaborate north wing of the Raadhuis at Gent (Fig. 6), also Late Gothic, for which he and de Waghemaekere were jointly responsible, though begun in 1518, the year after his work on the Palais de Savoie started, was not completed until four years after Keldermans's death in 1531. That, in any case, had no large gables as executed. Once, however, there were several modest gabled dormers (Fig. 83), now removed, and Keldermans's drawings propose one or two larger gables also (Fig. 7). Their design is quite unrelated to those under way in these years on the Palais de Savoie.

South of the Schelde two notable Early Renaissance facades of the mid-1530s, just when that portion of the Gent Raadhuis which Keldermans and de Waghemaekere built was being completed, still survive largely in their original condition, one at Mechelen and an-other at Brugge. The house called *De Zalm* (the salmon), at Zontwerf 5 on the bank of the Dijle in Mechelen, preserves three main storeys from the early or mid-sixteenth century. Above, the existing gable is mostly, if not wholly, the product of a later remodeling, so that the facade need be only briefly considered here. Long ago, the date of this house was set as early as 1519 by Paul Clemen. That dating was based on his assumption the sculpture was by Jan Borremans, who had already become a citizen of Brussels in 1479. Now a date in the early 1530s is accepted as more probable.[75] The front is a direct translation of the sort of Late Gothic facades that can be seen today on several of the guild-houses, as "restored" since the war, on the north side of the Groote Markt at Antwerp (Fig. 66) and along the Graslei in Gent (Figs. 18, 19). It is, however, much more richly decorated with carving in stone than the similarly translated facades of De Fonteine of 1539 in Gent (Fig. 26) or the Antwerp Wewershuis (Fig. 24) of a few years later.

The front of the *Griffie* (hall of records) in the Burg at Brugge (Fig. 25)—which is more securely attributed than De Zalm both as to date and authorship—is crowned with decorative scrolling of a rather idiosyncratic sort. Designed probably as early as 1534 or 1535[76] by Jean Wallot, this was completed in 1537 by the master-mason Christian (Chrétien) Six-deniers,[77] so that it is contemporary with the work of Vincidor and Pasqualini at Breda and IJsselstein. The *parti* is much the same as for the Zalmhuis; but the facade is broader, lower, and much less regular. The scrolled gables over the side bays look as if they were enlarged and corrupted versions of Pasqualini's earlier gablets over the Breda outworks and the later ones in the court there (Figs. 20, 22, 23), which last may well be precisely contemporary. The taller one in the middle, subsuming three bays, also has bold scrolling; but there is no evident relationship to the scrolled and pedimented Serlian gable Pasqualini introduced at this time —or more probably a few years later—at Buren (Fig. 29) which will shortly be described. The Brugge facade certainly owes nothing to Serlio, whose Book IV of *Architectura*, the first to be published, was only just appearing in Venice in 1537.

There are two stages on the middle gable at Brugge and, in its center, a high window flanked by spirally fluted columns. This, and all the windows of the front of the Griffie, are subdivided by stone mullions and transoms which lend a rather Tudor air to the whole. The arch over the tiny entrance door is still four-centered and pointed; however, that over the broad gateway in the right-hand bay is flattened and three-centered like the central arch on the north side of the court of the Palais de Savoie.

This extraordinary front of the Brugge Griffie is hard to place in any international sequence. Its faintly English flavor is presumably coincidental, while the suggestion of Sanmichele that some see in the spiral fluting of the columns flanking the window in the central gable is surely as improbable an actual influence as any from across the North Sea.[78] All the same, the provincial corruption of the detailing is matched here in the southern Netherlands by that of the ranges of stubby and bulbous baluster elements supporting the four-centered arches that run all around the vast, and nearly contemporary, arcaded court of the *Palais des Princes-Évêques* (prince-bishops palace) at Liège. This was begun for the prince-bishop Erard Cardinal de la Marck as early as 1526[79] by Aert van der Mulcken, but work continued over a decade or more. Similar but less corrupt, in execution at least, is the arcade of 1545 at the base of the *Spaansche Gouvernement* (seat of Habsburg rule) at Maastricht[80] in Dutch Limburg.

Quite unlike the very exceptional facade of the Griffie in Brugge is that of De Fonteine in Gent, which carries in the central lunette of the lowest stage of the gable the date 1539.[81] The ground storey has been destroyed to provide a modern shop window, but the upper storey and the gable, though the brickwork is stuccoed and painted today, as are also the stone mullions, preserve their original character. The storeys below the gable are fronted by a grid with maximal window openings. The lunettes over the windows are not semi-elliptical, however, as they had usually been before this in the line of descent from Brabantine Late Gothic, but half-round.

The other most advanced feature of De Fonteine, particularly in relation to the international development of the scrolled gable, is the treatment of the edges of the four crowning stages. Nothing quite like this had been seen later than the northern wings of the Palais de Savoie (Figs. 11, 12), though the concave C-scrolls on the third stage do almost match those on the Metselaershuis here of 1527 (Fig. 18). The bottom stage has S-scrolls and three double windows under the lunettes just like those on the storeys below. The shallow second stage includes the lunettes of the windows in the first stage, while only one window occupies the third stage. The fourth stage links C-scrolls to S-scrolls by short vertical members and is topped by a tiny pedimented edicule with straight vertical sides.

The Griffie in Brugge was altogether exceptional; the facade of the De Fonteine, whether or not the first of its kind, belongs to a line that extended in Gent down to the 1590s.[82] Two similar gables of 1564 on the Wenemaerhospital in the Sint-Verle-plein there will be illustrated later (Fig. 49). From the following year a facade even closer to that of De Fonteine is recorded in a drawing of 1869. Of a decade later than that was a nearly identical gable in the Koornmarkt, which is known both from another drawing and from old photographs taken before its demolition around 1887. Much later still is the house of 1590 called *De Kuip van Gent*, also in the Koornmarkt, with fewer stages and more generous scrolling on the gable. Various others are undated, such as the one known as *De Graven van Vlaanderen* at the corner of Burgstraat and the Gewad. Restored in the early twentieth century, this is unusually large and elaborate. Wreathed heads occupy all the lunettes, including those—all restorations—of the ground story, and the original brickwork, earlier stuccoed, is now exposed. Yet the succession of stages and the scrolled edges of the gables repeat once more those of De Fonteine. Finally, among more modest examples, is the house called *De Hazewind* in the Lange Munt, of which a drawing showing the original arcaded ground story is preserved in the city archive of Gent.

During the 1530s, while gables elaborated in outline either by sculptural decoration or by scrolls were being introduced on public and private works in Breda and in Gent, an architectonic sort of decorated gable very similar in character to the one over De Fonteine had already been introduced in Germany. At Neuburg-a.-d.-Donau in the Upper Palatinate the local Wittelsbach ruler, the Count Palatine Ottheinrich, was extending his Schloss with new west, south, and north wings employing the Nürnberger Hans Knotz. The work began about 1530, and all that Knotz would have been responsible for was completed by 1538.[83] The earlier gables on the west wing do not survive, but their design is known from a drawing made before they were removed in the early nineteenth century (Fig. 27). Quite unrelated to the simple *welsche Gebel* of lunette shape that were increasingly popular in Germany, these represent rather a translation into a basically *quattrocento* vocabulary of the reticulated Late Gothic gables of the early sixteenth century that long continued in common use throughout northern Europe. Nearly contemporary Flemish examples in Gent of 1527 and 1531 (Figs. 18, 19) have been discussed earlier. Innumerable German ones are certainly also of this general period even though most of them cannot be precisely dated.

The emphasis in the design of Knotz's Neuburg gables[84] had shifted, however, from the vertical patterns of the Late Gothic gables to the horizontal. Each of the five stages was topped by a modest entablature and the pilasters of the related arch orders were discontinuous from stage to stage though lined up one above another. At the edges, pairs of small C-scrolls on each stage provided a scalloped outline, but this scrolling is still timid compared to that on the gables of the Palais de Savoie (Figs. 11, 12) or the sculptural elaboration of those on the Breda Kasteel (Fig. 22).

The surviving gables and gabled dormers on the north wing at Neuburg,[85] completed by 1538 before Knotz's departure, were probably designed by him three or four years at least after those on the west wing. These are much bolder in design and no longer have any resemblance to Late Gothic examples (Fig. 18). The end gables each have four rather than five stages, with only three on those of the dormers; and the strong horizontals—string-courses rather than entablatures—between the stages are not associated with pilaster orders. What is most notable, and may properly be considered advanced internationally, are the vigorous curves of the scrolls at the ends of each stage. The second and fourth stages have S-scrolls wound into tight spirals at their upper termination; on the lowest stage convex and concave C-scrolls are linked by short verticals; while in the third stage this is simplified to unscrolled C-quadrants below straight verticals. The crowning element is a small lunette rather than a triangular pediment and thus is similar to contemporary and earlier *welsche Gebel* (Fig. 5).

DUTCH GABLES OF THE 1540S AND 1550S

By the early 1540s gable design in the northern Netherlands was beginning to catch up with German work of the period such as Knotz's at Neuburg. Conspicuous in Arnhem, near the present German border, is still the *Duivelshuis* (devil's house), the local name for the headquarters of the general of the Gelderland forces, Maerten van Rossum. This was built around 1540–46 and has lately been restored as a wing (Fig. 28) of the new postwar Raadhuis. The plain stepped gables of the surviving gatehouse of Maerten's mansion in Zaltbommel, dating from the mid-1530s, were not used here. Instead, the gablets of the dormers over the main block, basically sharp triangles, were elaborated by scrolling—now renewed by the restorers—in the same way as were the dormers on the Kasteel at Breda (Fig. 23). More significantly, the gablets crowning the tower on the right, which do not front dormers but are purely decorative and even pierced by oculi, have bolder scrolls at the sides. They are capped, moreover, with entablatures and pediments in a manner that may almost be considered Serlian.

Not unrelated to both sorts of gablets at Arnhem was the bigger gable on the Kasteel at Buren in Gelderland (Fig. 29), where Pasqualini was working for the last local lord, Floris van Egmond, in the 1530s and into the 1540s. This can more justifiably be called Serlian, even though Serlio's woodcut that might have provided the specific model—the gateway at the rear of his design for a *scena tragica* (Fig. 30)—was published in France only in 1545.[86] By that time Floris van Egmond was dead and Pasqualini's work at Buren had presumably come to an end. But Pasqualini might have remembered something comparable from his early years in Bologna, whether by Serlio himself or another architect.

Practically nothing survives of the Kasteel at Buren, of which the rule passed to the house of Nassau with William of Orange's marriage to Anna van Egmond, the heiress of Floris. But the extant octagonal lantern over the crossing of the church there suggests Pasqualini's hand by its resemblance to the IJsselstein tower that he built, probably also for Floris, in the 1530s. Fortunately, there exists an eighteenth-century drawing of the court of the Buren Kasteel (Fig. 29). This drawing indicates that the side wings were of a vernacular simplicity, with a variety of pointed, stepped, and hooded dormers breaking the roofs. However, the way the main block ran between two square towers faintly recalls the composition of Serlio's chateau of Ancy-le-Franc in France, already projected but not yet begun.[87]

In the center of the court front of this block at Buren, as seen in the drawing, a projection —possibly rusticated but more probably banded in brick and stone—terminates in a large gable. That gable was evidently much more proto-Academic in character than the ones on Ottheinrich's north wing that may be nearly contemporary or possibly a few years earlier. On this Buren gable the main stage was flanked by pilasters, beyond which were very bold S-scrolls; it was then capped with an entablature and a pediment of lower and more "correct" pitch than that of 1532 on the outworks at Breda (Fig. 20). The scrolling dolphins on the slopes of the pediment are hardly Serlian. Rather they repeat, as on the Duivelshuis (Fig. 28) at about this time, a motif that Pasqualini first used at Breda for the gablets on the outworks—one later emulated there atop the facades in the main court, which are otherwise so High Renaissance in character (Figs. 21, 23).

The Buren gable cannot be more precisely dated than before 1545, the year of Floris van Egmond's death. On the gabled dormer above the central bay of the facade of the Raadhuis at Utrecht, however, known to have been begun by Willem van Noort[88] in 1547, Pasqualini's

Buren gable design was repeated in the terminal stage above a pilaster-flanked window in the stage below (Fig. 31). Moreover, the right-hand end of this structure, notable otherwise for the profusion of *quattrocento* detail on the three successive pilaster orders of the five-bay front, carried a much larger version of what may loosely be called the Serlian gable.

On another, probably somewhat earlier, work of the 1540s, of which a portion of the comparably rich facade may be what still survives at Waterstraat 26 in Zaltbommel, the house of Maerten van Rossum's brother, Jan or Johan, scrolled gables that are no more to be considered Serlian than Knotz's at Neuburg once existed in some profusion. An early drawing preserved in the Stadarchief at Arnhem makes evident that this mansion was a rambling affair and more than probably erected in several successive campaigns (Fig. 32). On the left the three gables that crown a double bay of the facade and the two single bays at its side have what seem, in the drawing, to be pairs of scrolling dolphins such as were introduced on gablets at Breda and Arnhem in the 1530s and early 1540s (Figs. 20–23, 28). These creatures flank on each gable a single applied colonnette surmounted by an entablature block carrying a figure with a flag. Even below the gables, this facade was evidently extremely elaborate. But the decorative detail must have resembled that surviving on Maerten van Rossum's gatehouse at Zaltbommel of some years earlier more than that on his contemporary Duivelshuis at Arnhem or on the Utrecht Raadhuis (Figs. 28, 31).

The larger right-hand portion of Johan's mansion as that once stood in Zaltbommel is considerably less regular than the portion on the left; it is also more simply treated as regards the framing of the windows, though these were all topped with round bearing arches. This portion carries, however, scrolled gables over all three of its articulated wings. These gables were evidently far closer to Knotz's of the mid to late 1530s on the north wing at Neuburg (Fig. 16) than to anything now known of earlier date in the Netherlands. Two of the gables are staged, with horizontal string-courses that delimit the stages in contrast to the verticalism of the gables on the left. Moreover, the stages are framed with relatively bold S-scrolls below and C-scrolls above, thus producing a scalloped outline.

The accidental survival of a visual document recording this remarkable facade at Zaltbommel suggests there may once have been other equally early examples of scrolled gables in the north that were as advanced in their design but were never recorded. Such might well have existed in various, then larger, cities which have like Amsterdam been mostly rebuilt since the sixteenth century, to rival those at Neuburg (Fig. 16); indeed, scrolled gables have just been mentioned at Utrecht (Fig. 31), though those were probably a few years later than Johan van Rossum's. Unexpected, certainly, would be influence in the Netherlands from Germany in this period. But there does exist a rather tenuous biographical link since William of Orange, after the death of Anna van Buren, married the sister of the Elector Moritz of Saxony. Some Dutchman might have seen the scrolled gables of the 1540s on the Dresden

Residenzschloss;[89] however, the rather Serlian ones there probably date from after 1547, when Moritz became elector of Saxony, the same year van Noort began the Utrecht Raadhuis. Knowledge of the Neuburg gables is altogether less likely. The most probable models would have been gables like the one on De Fonteine of 1539 (Fig. 26) at Gent if such were seen by Dutchmen at this point.

It is curious, however, that after the one on the Griffie in Brugge (Fig. 25)—a most exceptional work—and the one in Gent (Fig. 26) very few scrolled gables dating certainly or probably from these years can be found today either in Flanders or in Brabant. Parent does illustrate, however, one in Brugge on the Sint Joris-straat dated 1544,[90] five years after De Fonteine, which was still standing in 1926. In Antwerp the extensive destruction of the Groote Markt in the 1570s, especially the north side, in the fire set by the Spaniards may well be the explanation. Earlier facades on the guildhouses in the square might have had scrolled gables, as several did later in the century and many after 1600. The only surviving front in the Groote Markt of these years—that of the Wewershuis on the north side which is dated in the early 1540s (Fig. 24)—does not have a scrolled gable. The gable is staged, however, and the pediment of the central window edicule in the upper stage breaks through the slanting lines of the sides to provide a slightly articulated crown.

Antwerp was the metropolis of northern Europe in the early sixteenth century and, from the 1550s and 1560s, design books published there had a very widespread influence on architecture. It already had a leading position in the introduction of Renaissance design in the Netherlands, particularly as regards painting.[91] Utrecht, however, was the seat of a bishop who became, thanks to the insistence of Charles V, the first northern pope as Adrian VI, and that city was at least as cosmopolitan as Antwerp. This the Raadhuis there makes evident. In these mid-century decades few Dutch buildings had so much arabesque decoration. Arnhem, the principal city in Gelderland, was and is a considerable urban entity; but Zaltbommel, though a port on the Waal—as the Rhine is called where it flows through Holland—is by contrast only a town and Buren but a village. Advanced design was evidently not limited to the bigger cities of the day.

Culemborg, in fact, where the most advanced Dutch gable of the late 1540s survives, is like Buren only a small town to the north of Zaltbommel on the Lek, geographically in the province of Gelderland today. In the Middle Ages it was not a part of that duchy but the seat of a succession of local counts. As at Buren, the male line died out in the early sixteenth century leaving an heiress, Elizabeth van Culemborg. She married as her second husband Antoine de Lalaing, count of Hoogstraten in south Brabant, who had employed Rombout Keldermans in the mid-1520s to build for him at Hoogstraten Sint Katerina. That church was eventually brought to completion with the construction of the tower in 1546, long after Rombout's and Antoine's deaths in 1531 and 1540, respectively, but before Elizabeth's in

1555. The Culemborg Raadhuis, though not erected until 1534-39, reputedly follows a design provided by Keldermans.

This modest municipal building in Culemborg, of brick sparsely banded in stone, is in a simple version of Rombout's Brabantine Late Gothic. There is no more infiltration of Italian elements in the detail than on the structure he began at Mechelen for the Grand Council toward 1530 or his wing of the Raadhuis at Gent (Fig. 6), which was, in 1535, just reaching completion at the hands of Waghemaekere after his death. Specifically, the windows have semi-elliptical heads filled with cusped tracery in contrast to the *quattrocento* design of those on Maerten van Rossum's contemporary gatehouse at Zaltbommel and Het Hemelrijk in Mechelen, and their glazing does not have any of the Renaissance character of the stained glass of 1528-35 in the church at Hoogstraten. Moreover, the gables, stepped like the ones that survive at Zaltbommel, are elaborated with spirally fluted finials of distinctly Late Gothic character. Above all, there is no reflection whatever of the north wing of the Palais de Savoie as that was completed by Keldermans almost a decade earlier (Figs. 11, 12, 17).

Despite the local link with its builder, however, there seems no reason to suppose that the remarkable facade of the house at Markt 11 in Culemborg either, now occupied by the Amsterdam-Rotterdam Bank (Fig. 33), at all reflects the Palais de Savoie. Though dated 1549, however, the flavor is almost as *quattrocento* as that of a more metropolitan work, van Noort's nearly contemporary Raadhuis at Utrecht (Fig. 31). In the blind arcade of the upper storey the arches are semi-elliptical, and their molded archivolts rise from paneled Ionic pilasters. These rest on scrolled *ressauts* at the top of the ground story. Above, the lunettes over the heads of the windows in the gable have shell fluting and there are even coin-like medallions above them.

Compared with the bold scrolls flanking the gables at Buren and Utrecht, not to speak of those on the ones over the right half of the Johan van Rossum house at Zaltbommel (Figs. 29, 31, 32), the scrolls outlining the three stages of the gable at Culemborg seem flaccid and attenuated (Fig. 33). Moreover, the spiraling lower ends of the S-scrolls on the first stage and the C-scrolls on the second stage—there are none in the top stage—look as underscaled as those of the 1490s by Meo di Caprino on Turin Cathedral. That underscaling contrasts with the considerable size and the high relief of the carved heads which are set into the lower stage and at the center of the middle stage, as well as providing the crowning element of the terminal lunette.

Only in the slight hint of strapwork in the framing of the date stones inscribed "1549" is there any suggestion on this facade at Culemborg of the new Northern Mannerist ornament. Such ornament, of which strapwork was a principal ingredient often combined with elements of grotesque, seems to have been first introduced—at least at architectural scale and in some profusion—that very year. It appeared as cresting over various features, other-wise conventionally arched and pilastered, in the street decorations designed by Cornelis Floris de Vriend[92] for the ceremonial entrée of Charles and his son Philip into Antwerp (Fig. 34). These were published by Pieter Coecke in 1550 and may, some scholars believe, have been by Coecke himself rather than by Floris.[93] That seems unlikely, however, except possibly for the title-page (Fig. 35). But, although the title-page is book decoration, not a representation of anything actually built, however temporary, the ornament on it was soon copied in architectural detailing as much as that on other plates in the volume.

The mixture of advanced and retarded details in the carved elements on the Culemborg facade seems only too characteristic of provincial work; yet, if judged as a total entity, this gable is the most advanced for the date of any that seem to be extant today in either the northern or the southern Netherlands. Surely others must once have existed, as noted earlier, especially in the larger towns and cities.

Very soon, indeed, much bolder and more coherent examples of scrolled gables were appearing in the northern Netherlands to rival contemporary German examples. Zierikzee is a small port in the province of Zeeland, on the Gouwe between the islands of Schouven and Duiveland beside the Ooster Schelde. Between 1550 and 1554 the modest Raadhuis there was being rebuilt beside the surviving tower of the fourteenth-century *Vleeshal* (meat market). On the front of this toward the street, which is all of stone, two gables rise side by side, breaking the eaves of the transverse main roof behind them (Fig. 36). The large pedi-mented windows are eighteenth-century emendations; but the edges of the gables, although by comparison to the gable of the house in Culemborg very simply detailed, have a series of vigorous curves outlining the three stages. (Or should it be considered four, since the upper face of the main wall is brought forward below the gables and this plane is then carried up over the line of the main eaves?) The next stage, above a stringcourse, has convex quadrants followed by straight verticals, as on the third stage of the end gables of the north wing at Neuburg-a.-d.-Donau that date from some fifteen or so years earlier (Fig. 16). The penulti-mate stage is flanked by concave quadrants, while a plain semicircular lunette above crowns a much simplified entablature. The only carved decoration consists of circular medallions of Charles V and his son Philip inset in the lunettes.

The *speeltoren* (carillon tower) at Zierikzee on the Raadhuis should also be mentioned, although its bells, cast between 1550 and 1554 by Petrus van den Gheyn, are now elsewhere. It is the oldest surviving example of the elaborately staged Dutch spires[94] that are a sort of three-dimensional parallel to the scrolled gables. The next oldest, and much taller and more elaborate, is far to the east in Gdańsk, but carried out by a Dutchman, Daniel Dirksen, in 1559–60.[95] In the northern Netherlands no other survives earlier than the one at Edam, in the province of Noord Holland, which is of 1568–69. Many more, however, once existed and were rebuilt after fires in the seventeenth century following the earlier models. That at Monnikendam, moreover, actually dates in its present form from 1591. It is evident that these were from the first civic monuments not, as might be expected, adjuncts to churches. The prominent freestanding *Munttoren* in the center of Amsterdam dates from the late fifteenth century, but was carried much higher in 1620 by Hendrick de Keyser (1565-1621).

From the mid-sixteenth-century decades little survives in Amsterdam. Vastly increased prosperity and attendant architectural production came there only after the Schelde was closed and international trade shunted from Antwerp to the expanding Dutch port. However, of the front of the *Bushuis* (arsenal), built almost simultaneously with the Zierikzee Raadhuis in 1555, there is an old photograph as well as a seventeenth-century engraving and an eighteenth-century drawing (Fig. 37).[96] Though both the engraver and the draftsman were evidently more interested in the broader and grander facade next door of what must be the later *Oost Indisch Huis*, the character of the successive stages of the Bushuis gable can, with some difficulty, be made out. The lowest stage was effectively the top story of the building and had a range of four large windows identical with those of the story below. However, the edges were outlined by tall concave curves above short vertical elements, as the story below of course was not.

The next stage of the Bushuis gable was considerably shallower, and the four windows in it could not be as tall as those below. Again, there were concave curves at the sides; in this case short C-scrolls with spiraled ends. The following, also very shallow, stage was blind and the C-curves at its edges more tightly spiraled. The terminal stage, wholly decorative, was open in the center between two rather timid "horns" of S-curvature. Vigorous string-courses at sill level set the stages apart, and above the mullioned and transomed windows stone voussoirs in relief alternated with brick bands. The surface of the penultimate stage carried carved ornament, but of what sort it is difficult to judge from either the drawing or the photograph.

The development of Mannerist ornament, of the northern sort later so much used on scrolled gables not only in the Netherlands but throughout northern Europe, was in any case not yet very far advanced even in the Netherlands. Initiated in the late 1540s by Cornelis Floris or, less probably, by Pieter Coecke, it had not been made generally available on more than a fairly small number of engraved plates (Fig. 34) until Floris published in Antwerp in 1556 and 1557 the two volumes of his *Weeldeley niewe Inventien van Antijcksche* (Fig. 38). Even after that his inventions were rarely adopted in architectural design for some years. Floris himself did not employ his newly elaborated ornament[97] on the Antwerp Raadhuis of 1561-65 (Figs. 45, 46) if, indeed, he was the responsible designer of that major monument as well as superintendent during its construction.[98] In these same years, however, a disciple who signed "H. H." (probably Hendrick Haggart) did introduce such decoration, though not very conspicuously, on the sculptured tomb-edicule of Edo Wiemken at Jever[99] in northwestern Germany. Moreover, it is not very prominent, if present at all, on the considerable number of scrolled gables surviving in the northern Netherlands from the two decades following the mid-century (Figs. 36–61).

Throughout northern Europe urban public edifices were becoming more important architecturally in relation to the Schlösser, kasteelen, and more modest country houses local rulers and landowners were building. Nowhere was this more true than in the northern Netherlands. There even such leading figures of the day as Maerten van Rossum built their residences in towns like Arnhem or Zaltbommel, not on estates in the country. Just as, by contrast, Somerset House on the Strand in London, when erected in the 1540s, was an exception in England, by being a city mansion, since great houses there were usually erected in the country, so in Holland, Huis Twickel, which is not in a town but in the country well outside of Delden, a small place to the south of Almelo in Overijsel, is unusual though not unique in this period.

Though Huis Twickel is comparable in size and regularity of design more to contemporary French chateaux than to Tudor country houses, it contributed little to Netherlandish architectural development. This is particularly true as regards gable design. The gable above the entrance on the front, carrying the date 1551, projects from a long hip roof of similar pitch (Fig. 39). Though subdivided into three stages marked by string-courses, the sides are straight and slanted to the slope of the roof. The outline is broken only by the curious projections at the ends of the string-courses. These elements, perhaps intended as bases for statuary, are supported on small scroll-brackets that do not change the outline of the gable as a whole. Only the two stone dormers flanking the central gable have C-scrolls with spiraling ends. These are set below small pediments filled with fluting. Thus the Twickel dormers recall the gabled ones on the Palais de Savoie of a generation earlier—and hence, ultimately, those of the chateaux of the Loire—more than they do such contemporary Dutch scrolled gables as have just been described. Below, however, right over the portal, minor elements of rising concave curvature frame the conspicuous armorial panel. Town buildings, both public and private, are more typical than this country house of the 1550s.

The somewhat later *Weeshuis* (guildhall) at Edam of 1558[100] is not extant. However, an eighteenth-century drawing (Fig. 40) makes fairly clear the design of the gable that once rose over the central three bays of its seven-bay front. As seen in the drawing, there are on the lowest stage of the gable—which is carried straight up from the face of the attic—three large mullioned and transomed windows under round bearing arches. The arches evidently had stone imposts and keystones set in the brickwork of the walls. Above the top of the attic the edges of the lowest stage had simple members, also of stone, that were S-shaped rather than merely concave curves as on the Amsterdam Bushuis (Fig. 37). Both the second and the third stage were edged with similar curves carried out in brick, and a plain pediment provided the terminal feature.

From the next year, 1559, several scrolled gables still exist in Holland. That on the so-called *Kardinalshuis* (Fig. 41), of which the facade has been rebuilt at the left end of the *Provincie Huis* in Groningen, is in outline the least advanced and, despite its small dimensions, the most elaborate. The engaged columns between the exceptionally large rectangular windows of the two stories are repeated to flank the large central window in the main stage of the gable. Narrower side bays are flanked by pilasters, Corinthian and fluted like the engaged columns, and carry rondels with heads in high relief not unlike those on Markt 11 in Culemborg (Fig. 33) of a decade earlier. In the next very shallow stage there is a third such head and the inscription giving the date. Rectangular shapes dominate, but beyond the pilasters of the lower stage there are rather bold S-scrolls below vertical elements. On the next stage the reclining *putti* on the ends of the cornice of the Corinthian order are much more conspicuous than the tiny S-scrolls farther in, while the concave curves below the terminal pediment are almost invisible.

Several things are novel about this Groningen facade: On the one hand, there is the attempt to coordinate the treatment of the gable with the columnar articulation of the facade below—what may, in exaggeration, be called the Dutch High Renaissance aspect—on the other hand, there is the Northern Mannerist aspect represented, if still rather timidly, by the introduction of ornamental elements that seem to be related to those in the plates of Floris's *Inventien* (Fig. 38). Most striking is the ornate carving that covers the lower third of the Doric order of the ground story below the fluting and, on the gable itself, the bold but flat strapwork carved on the surface of the scrolls flanking the main stage. Even more Floris-like is the strapwork in relief around the cartouches below the heads occupying the rondels. Within these cartouches, the inscription on that to the right reads "Carolus Magnus"; on the one to the left, "Alexander [?] Magnus," grander patrons than Charles and Philip on the Raadhuis at Zierikzee.

Even more impressive, however, and quite devoid of Northern Mannerist ornament, are the two gables over the inner side of a slightly later structure, a city-gate at Zierikzee, the *Noordhavenpoort* (Fig. 42), which also carry the date 1559. The wall below the gables is pierced by a great plain arch detailed only with a bevel on the intrados. This wall is of roughly squared rubble, like the Raadhuis here of the first years of the decade, and probably a survival from an earlier structure on the site of which much is still extant behind. The wall was now finished off, however, with four courses of fine ashlar masonry crowned with an extremely elegant entablature. That is repeated, moreover, at the top of each of the three stages of the gables. In the center of both gables are large mullioned and transomed windows flanked by very delicate paneled pilasters associated with the entablature above. Over each of the windows is a pediment, detailed as crisply as the entablature. The second stage of the two gables is edged with C-scrolls. These have spiraling inner and outer ends that echo the ones on the short convex C-scrolls flanking the base of the main stage. The third stage is severely rectangular with no scrolling, and the topmost a lunette of somewhat vertical proportion.

Elements at architectural scale dominate the composition of these gables on the Noordhavenpoort almost as much as on those, so differently organized, of the earlier town hall here (Fig. 36). At that scale, too, are the balls, raised on short tapered shanks, that accent both ends of all the entablatures, and also the oculi in the third stage of the gables. But there is also a certain amount of more detailed carving: small heads in bold relief, somewhat as at Groningen, set low within wreaths on the first stage and two more, similarly wreathed, in the lunettes at the top. More conspicuous here, in contrast to the light-colored stone, are the ornamental ends of the black iron ties and the figures of the date 1559, also of black iron, two digits to each gable.

The almost High Renaissance character of the Zierikzee gables that results from the particular proportions and, even more, from the refinement of the detailing—rather than, as at Groningen, from the use of applied orders—is not at all reflected in the gables of the precisely contemporary *Waag* (weigh house) at Enkhuizen (Fig. 43), a former fishing port on the IJsselmeer in the province of Noord Holland. There is very little carved decoration here except for the five free-standing allegorical statues of Justice, Faith, Hope, Love, and Force mounted in pairs on the gable at the right end and alone in the middle of the long side, but the general flavor is provincial Northern Mannerist, indeed almost vernacular. It is the irregularity of the lower walls, doubtless incorporating earlier construction, that gives the building as a whole its rather rustic charm thanks particularly to the varied sizes and shapes of the doors and windows, the brightly painted shutters, and the small accents of white stone that recur throughout.

Formal design on the Enkhuizen Waag begins only with the broad friezelike member that tops the lower walls. This is articulated by the paneled podia of the five statues and decorated by coats of arms carved on square stone panels and polychromed. In the center of each facade at this level there is a blind arch, banded with occasional small voussoirs of stone, which is filled with a fluted lunette. These arches and lunettes are repeated in the tall first stages of the gables above broad openings with the same painted wooden shutters as on the larger windows below. More striking, and at far bolder scale, are the stone scrolls in pairs edging the sides of each of the gables. The lower scrolls have tightly spiraled ends; the smaller ones above are simply S-curved. However, the upper scrolls are tied into the face of the gable by plain stone blocks. These are mounted on carved bosses that project between the lower and the upper pairs. Above, there are square urns that look like lanterns. Over a vigorous cornice, the next stage is plainer, but here the S-scrolls on the first stage below are repeated and the gable on the end has in the center one small oblong window. The terminal stage has again small S-scrolls at its base, above which straight vertical members lead up to the entablature below the crowning pediment. The frieze of this entablature carries decoration in low relief and the surfaces of all the scrolls are also decorated with inconspicuous foliate carving. At the base of the terminal edicules, however, heads in three dimensions project boldly from stone lozenges.

More important public edifices of this period once existed in Amsterdam, though nothing but the Bushuis seems to be documented visually even as well as that. However, the exterior of the *Paalhuis* dated 1560[101] beside the *Nieuwe Brug* (new bridge) on the Damrak is known from a seventeenth-century engraving and eighteenth-century watercolors (Fig. 44). Except for the arms in the central bay, there was on this structure little carved decoration comparable to that on the Enkhuizen Waag; but the general design of the two gables, though they differ from each other, is more advanced. That over the middle of the land side had no big scrolls, but over the pilasters at the sides of the main stage there was an entablature and a pediment. The end gable, on the other hand, has exceptionally bold S-scrolls on both the lower and the upper stages. The whole, all the same, though a civic and not a private commission, was modest in size even if once conspicuous because of its site near the center of Amsterdam.

V   Antwerp

THE RAADHUIS

UP TO THIS POINT most major public buildings in the Netherlands, unlike the Paalhuis, had either been carried forward like the Gent Raadhuis in the Brabantine Late Gothic in which they had been begun or, if like the Utrecht Raadhuis of Renaissance design, they were relatively modest in size, however elaborately detailed, and quite retardataire by Italian standards. But the vast Raadhuis of 1561–65,[102] most probably projected by Cornelis Floris, occupying the whole of the west side of the Groote Markt in Antwerp, still boldly proclaims today in the international language of the mid-century that city's commercial preëminence then in the north of Europe. It is a notable landmark for size and prominence alone (Fig. 45) since it extends nine and a half trabeated bays on the front to left and to right of a very tall central feature. That consists of three wider arched bays, here flanked by pairs of engaged columns rather than the flat pilasters which separate the mullioned and transomed windows of the ordinary bays.

The ground storey of the Antwerp Raadhuis is no more than a base, all rusticated, with low round-arched portals in the wings and semi-elliptical ones, more broadly spaced, in the center. Over this basement the two main storeys have orders standing on podia, Doric in the first storey, Ionic in the second. Above the second storey on the wings a balustraded gallery opens beneath the heavily modillioned cornice. In the center at this level comes the

49

lowest stage of the main gable, which has an additional order. That is as tall as those below and here properly Corinthian. Pairs of columns flank the central panel carved with the polychromed arms of the city. These columns are of marble like those that frame the niche above with its statue of the Virgin. The niches on the lower stage hold allegorical figures, and there is more armorial decoration on the piers beyond them.

The middle and top stages of the central projection on the Antwerp Raadhuis (Fig. 46) break with the regularity and horizontality of the lower facade to provide a lively outline. This is not exactly scrolled but, as on the gables of a generation earlier on the Kasteel at Breda (Fig. 22), there is a rather scroll-like elaboration here of the outline thanks to the introduction of three-dimensional sculpture at the edges[103]: centaurs in combat with giant serpents in the middle stage and winged horses on the next. Moreover, at this level sculptural herms take the place of the orders below, and the heavy pediment these support is crowned by two small scrolled members as well as by a pedestal that carries a carved eagle on a ball. The most striking elements of the gable composition, however, are not the sculptural ones but the very tall obelisks that rise from the entablature of the first stage, past the second stage, to stand out above sharp and clear against the sky.

The generally proto-Academic character of this facade, carried out over four years in the early 1560s, has led scholars to query whether it can have been the unaided work of Cornelis Floris. The intervention of an alien hand—possibly Italian but more probably French —has been hypothesized, especially for the design of the main stories of the central projection, a feature which does seem to recall the pavilion on the south wing of the chateau of Ecouen in France added by Jean Bullant in the previous decade. On the other hand, the narrowing second and third stages relate the composition as a whole rather to the new northern sort of elaborated gable design which was not used in Italy or even in France either then or earlier. The conspicuous employment of an order on the lowest stage of a gable, echoing those on the facade below, was no novelty by this date, at least in the northern Netherlands (Fig. 42); nor was the introduction of three-dimensional sculpture at the sides unknown, as was just noted. The most popular feature that was boldly exploited on the Antwerp Raadhuis for the first time—one especially popular in German lands in the later decades of the century and into the next—was the tall obelisk. Such would add piquant vertical accents to the outline of innumerable scrolled gables all over northern Europe from this time on. Novel ornament had made as yet hardly more than a token appearance (Fig. 41) on executed works of architecture in the Netherlands, north or south.

THE ORNAMENT OF FLORIS AND VREDEMAN

Even before the Antwerp Raadhuis was completed, however, there had come out in that city, with the imprint date 1563, a volume of twenty-seven ornamental plates for which the missing title *Architectura* is usually supplied as well as the place of publication, which is not given either on the engraved title page. These plates displayed a great deal of the sort of decoration now called Northern Mannerist as executed by Hieronymus Cock but invented by Jan Vredeman de Fries.[104] Vredeman had produced an earlier collection of eight plates of grotesque designs, *Grotteco in diverse manieren*, Antwerp, 1554, but those are not relevant in connection with scrolled gables. He was born in 1527 in Leeuwarden, capital of the province of Friesland in the north, but was active in the south at least from the mid-1550s; he also traveled over much of northern Europe in search of employment.[105] Vredeman's designs, although not for some years emulated on actual buildings even in the Netherlands, had a more potent and long-lasting influence all over northern Europe than Floris's plates of 1556–57, especially on gables, since for them he supplied actual models. That book of 1563, moreover, was followed by further Vredeman publications in the late 1560s, 70s, and 80s, and even after 1600, although these offered only a few more designs that were specifically for scrolled gables.

Vredeman's ornament is related to the sort Floris had developed by 1550. Such ornament a sculptor, reputedly a disciple of Floris, who at this point signed "Hein. H." (? Haggart) and not—as a decade later at Jever in northwestern Germany—merely "H. H.," had employed already in 1554. He introduced it to decorate the spandrels over the lower arches of his two-storied screen in the church at Oosterend in Friesland. That owed nothing directly to Floris's *Inventien* or Vredeman's *Architectura* since it was executed much too early; but it may reflect the sculptor's memory of Floris's designs for the imperial entrée of 1549, doubtless refreshed by a look at the published plates of the next year (Fig. 34).

In comparison with Floris's ornament, as presented in the *Inventien* of 1556–57 (Fig. 38), Vredeman's on the title-page of his *Architectura* of seven years later (Fig. 47) is less sculptural and more like the 1550 title-page that may be by Coecke (Fig. 35). Rather than Floris's plastic modeling of abstract elements, Vredeman's strapwork is for the most part in a single plane only slightly raised from the field, and its membering tends to be angular rather than curvilinear. What is significant here, however, is that Vredeman was providing designs that were intended for scrolled gables (Fig. 48). In these his flat strapwork creates the C-scrolls and S-scrolls of the outline, but it also extends inward on the face of the gable to join the flat frames that surround the windows. He also offered a wide choice of fantastic variants on the obelisk theme to enliven the skyline of gables.

In some instances the strapwork elements in Vredeman's designs are crossed by bands differentiated from the rest of the raised detail by a textural treatment. Though this treatment is indicated on his plates only by a regular pattern of small dots, it probably was the model for the chip-carved members of stone so frequently associated with gables designed and executed in the Vredeman spirit in Holland and, even more conspicuously, in

German lands. Paradoxically, indeed, what seem to be the earliest examples of chip-carved blocks of stone that survive are in Westphalia; but it must be significant that these are on work of around 1560 carried out for Erich of Brunswick-Calenberg. Erich had estates in Holland at Worden—a place not identifiable as such on modern maps, but probably Woerden[106]—and brought masons from there to work on his German Schlösser at Uslar and Hannoversch-Münden. A surviving fragment at Uslar carries the date 1559; the other was built from 1562 onward.[107] Later this treatment, introduced so early in the upper Weser valley, became a characteristic device of the so-called Weserrenaissance in that region and elsewhere in Westphalia. Beginning in the 1570s (and probably some years earlier) chip-carving continued well beyond 1600 to be equally popular in the Netherlands.

As has been noted earlier, Vredeman's influence is rarely evident in executed work in the Netherlands of the mid- and later 1560s, at least in any that is extant today either in the north or in the south. The gables of the Wenemaerhospital in Gent, dated 1564[108] (Fig. 49), do have S-scrolls of stone at the edges as on earlier facades in Gent (Fig. 26). However, these are not detailed as strapwork, nor is there any raised decoration in stone on the plain brick faces of the gables in the Vredeman manner. Only simple horizontal string-courses mark off the four stages of each below pedimental terminations as on De Fonteine of 1539 and other Gent housefronts of the midcentury and after. In the north it is a little later only, on the facade of *Huis Bethlehem* at Gorinchem (Fig. 50), which carries the inscribed date 1566, that bolder scrolling appears. But even there the Northern Mannerist ornament in the lunettes of the blind arches is not linked in Vredeman's way by strapwork elements to the big scrolls at the sides.

On a much larger and more conspicuous Dutch building, the *Raadhuis* in The Hague (Fig. 51), the slightly earlier gables, dated 1564 and 1565, respectively, are more elaborated but less advanced in design than those on the Gorinchem house. On the front, a range of pilasters in the upper storey possibly reflects the orders on the facade of the Antwerp Raadhuis, which was just reaching completion at this date. Over that, the entablature is carried forward on heavy and elaborately carved brackets above the pilasters. In this projecting plane of the facade a balustrade fronts a loggia set into the main stage of the gable. The balustrade also runs all the way across the two bays on the left-hand side. Pairs of arches topped by carved panels between engaged Ionic columns further articulate this main stage. The next, much narrower stage is flanked by pilasters with short scrolled elements beyond them; but over this the shrunken terminal stage carries only a plain pediment. What most enlivens the skyline is not the architectural framing but five freestanding statues that are presumably of the same allegorical subjects as at Enkhuizen (Fig. 43). One pair stand on the ends of the balustrade; two more are on top of the entablature of that main stage; and a fifth crowns a pedestal rising out of the crowning pediment. Having no loggia and being largely of brick rather than of stone like the front, the other gable on the left-hand side of the Hague Raadhuis is simpler and flatter; but scrolled elements again flank the face of the main stage as well as the one above.

VI Netherlandish Gables at Home and Abroad

GABLES OF THE 1560S

EXPORTATION of the scrolled gable, as of some other Netherlandish architectural elements, may have begun a few years before 1560, but from the early 1560s onward more notable examples have survived outside than inside the Netherlands. That the crowning stages erected in 1559–60 of the tower of the Town Hall in Gdańsk by the Dutchman Daniel Dirksen is the grandest surviving sixteenth-century speeltoren has already been noted. Parallel to this, but slightly later, is a series of nearby gabled facades in the great Baltic port that rival in interest anything extant today from this period in Holland, much less in Belgium. Particularly impressive on the main street, the Długa, is the house at No. 45 because it occupies a corner site (Fig. 52). This is also presumed to be the earliest, i.e., c. 1560.[109] All three stories of the long side and the two ends are articulated by Doric pilaster orders in stone, while a pair of free-standing columns flanks the portal opening on the Długa. The gables at both ends are in three stages, with another Doric pilaster order on the lower stage and an entablature over that above. Vigorous vertical S-scrolls flank the first stage, and, on the next, additional carved decoration elaborates the C-scrolls at the sides. The tiny pediment at the top rides on two further C-scrolls flanked by spiky obelisks. These last are the only elements that might indicate some acquaintance with Vredeman's designs—if, indeed, this house is late enough to do so as does not seem likely.

The front of a house at Długa 37 (Fig. 53) carries the more precise date 1563. Though narrower, the gable of this is much more boldly outlined and the whole more lavishly decorated, but not in a way that suggests direct or indirect influence from Vredeman, who came to Gdańsk only much later. The shafts of the pilaster orders on the three storeys are covered with carved ornament and figural reliefs occupy the panels below the windows. This excessive richness carries over on to the gable. However, the surfaces of the S-scrolls flanking its lower stage have foliate rather than strapwork carving as do the nearly circular C-scrolls on the second stage. The crown is not easily described: Three free-standing statues provide an open triangular accent against the sky, much as just before this at Enkhuizen (Fig. 43); those in The Hague (Fig. 51) are later in date by at least a year or two.

Who the designers of these houses in the Długa were is not known, but it would seem from their varying design that two men were involved, one very likely from Holland in the north, presumably Amsterdam, the other from Antwerp or elsewhere in Brabant in the south. Flanders would be a somewhat less likely source. For the principal public monument erected in Gdańsk in these years, the *Zielona Brama* (green gate) of 1563–68,[110] two different architect-builders are documented: Regnier (d. 1572) who had, indeed, come from Amsterdam, and Johann Kramer from Dresden. He was the son of Bastian Kramer, who enlarged the Dresden Residenzschloss so much for successive Saxon dukes in the 1530s, 40s, and later. However, though Kramer doubtless worked under his father on the Residenzschloss at least in the 50s, there is nothing Saxon about the Zielona Brama as executed (Fig. 54). It may be presumed, therefore, that Kramer followed Regnier's design; concerning Regnier, unfortunately, almost nothing is known, not even his first name.

As on the house at Długa 45 (Fig. 52), the two brick facades of the Zielona Brama—one facing the water on the east, the other closing in the Długi Targ, the square that terminates the Długa at that end—both have a pilaster order on the main storey, not Doric here but Ionic and fluted. The ground storey is all of stone with rusticated bands and four great arches. Each side of the Zielona Brama has three gables, one in the center, which is four bays wide in the first stage, and two more at the ends that are only two bays wide. That lowest stage has a pilaster order, repeating the relatively severe treatment of the storeys below in a way that recalls the facades of the house at Długa 45. The next stage, again with a pilaster order, is flanked on all the gables—at least as they have been restored since the war—by horizontal S-scrolls topped by convex C-curved elements. On the next stage concave elements rise only half-height, but simple strapwork might suggest some early knowledge of Vredeman's designs of 1563 as the gable of Huis Bethlehem (Fig. 50) does not. The strapwork links the central oculi to the edges, as it does also on the terminal stage. This last is flanked by S-scrolls and topped with a small pediment and a statue. The vertical accent of the statue is echoed below by pairs of obelisks and urns.

In seeking Regnier's Dutch sources there is one public building in Amsterdam, dated 1560[111] like the Paalhuis, that might be considered. The facade of the *Burgerweeshuis* (guildhall) there, as known from a drawing (Fig. 55) of 1725 preserved in the Gemeente Archief in Amsterdam, had pilaster orders on the two main storeys and both stages of the gable. There were, in between, even larger windows, subdivided by stone mullions and transoms, than those in the main storey of the Zielona Brama. The first stage of the gable was, as in Gdańsk, rectangular though flanked by parapets with armorial carving. The terminal stage, however, pilastered and capped by an entablature and a plain pediment, did have scrolling elements at the sides. Like the southwest gable of a generation earlier on the Breda Kasteel (Fig. 22) and those to the right on the Johan van Rossum house in Zaltbommel (Fig. 32), these were made up of animal paws and knees. There is at this early date no Vredeman ornament, of course. The sculptured heads in rondels on the first stage of the gable recall rather those of the previous year on the Kardinalshuis at Groningen (Fig. 41). They also provide possible models for the carved motifs on the first stage of the main gables of the Zielona Brama (Fig. 54). These are carried out in three-dimensional Northern Mannerist bandwork. That bandwork seems already to lean a little on Floris if not, at this early date, on Vredeman. His *Architectura* dates, of course, from 1563, the very year the Zielona Brama was begun.

One of the finest German houses of the 1560s, the *Roter Ochse* in Erfurt in Thuringia (Fig. 56), which carries the date 1562,[112] has some likeness to contemporary work in Gdańsk. But there was here no close commercial tie with the Netherlands as in the Baltic port; nor are any such Dutchmen as Dirksen and Regnier, in this period, and the Van den Blockes and Anthonis van Opbergen, later, documented as working there. The very different materials, not brick and stone as in Holland and in Gdańsk but stucco rendering—boldly polychromed with paint in the latest restoration—make a quite dissimilar impression. Particularly, moreover, the pedimented windows of the main storey do not at all resemble the large unframed Dutch fenestration common to the Burgerweeshuis and the Zielona Brama (Figs. 55; 54). But the pilaster order of that storey and the additional pilaster orders on the two stages of the gable—not to speak of the scrolling sea-horses with foliate tails flanking the top stage as at Breda and Arnhem (Figs. 22, 28)—do suggest the Netherlands. The curious mixture of devils and scrolls in the plastic decorations flanking the lower stage of the gable has no close Netherlandish parallels, but the three-dimensional strapwork could be a crude echo of Floris's ornament; it is too early to reflect Vredeman's.

Whoever may have designed the facade of the Roter Ochse—a Dutchman or a German actually trained in Antwerp like Jürgen Crossmann[113] of Lemgo in this period—many Netherlanders were being employed on architectural design elsewhere in Germany by the late 1550s and 1560s, more than there had ever been Italians. Arndt Johannssen, the city architect of Arnhem, was in charge of the construction of Schloss Horst from 1558 to 1567 for Lüttger von der Horst, the lay deputy of the elector-archbishops of Cologne. The year before, a designer who signed "C. F.," presumably Cornelis Floris, made two projects for the *Doxal* (porch) of the Rathaus in Cologne.[114] It was on one of these that Wilhelm Vernukken (d. 1607), who was associated with Johannssen at Horst from around 1560, based much later the executed structure. Moreover, it was in 1558 that Ottheinrich von der Pfalz, the Elector Palatine, in the last year of his life called the sculptor Alexander Colin (c. 1528–1612)[115] from Mechelen to work on his new *Ottheinrichsbau* wing of the Heidelberg Schloss. The presence of Dutch workmen at Uslar from 1559 and a little later at Hannoversch-Münden has been mentioned, as also the Wiemken tomb at Jever, begun by H. H. (Hendrick Hagart?), who was certainly a Netherlander and probably from Antwerp, in 1561.

In 1563 another sculptor, Antonis van Zerroen, was called from Antwerp to execute, following the design of the German goldsmith Hans Wessel of Lübeck, the greater part of the carved decoration on the cenotaph of the Elector Moritz of Saxony in the Freiberg Münster.[116] The client was Moritz's brother and successor August. In this case a family link with the Netherlands existed, for their sister Anna, as earlier noted, was the second wife of the Dutch stadholder William of Orange. August employed another presumed Netherlander, Erhart van der Meer, at Schloss Augustusburg,[117] though the extent of his responsibility is no clearer than where he originally came from. Van der Meer had worked earlier on the Schloss at Arnstadt in Thuringia, but very little of that survives.

Sculptural production by Netherlanders abroad is more precisely documented than architectural employment. Among the various tombs by Floris and his followers in German lands the most notable is the one, dated 1568–74, of Duke Albrecht of Prussia in Königsberg (Kaliningrad)[118] and the big monument of the Landgrave Philip of Hesse[119] at Kassel. The latter was carried out, not by disciples of Floris, but by two Walloons from Cambrai—Elie Godefroy, before his death in 1568, and Adam Liquir Beaumont, who brought it to completion in 1572. These tombs offer no clues as to possible Netherlandish contributions to later scrolled gable design in Germany. Only the gables at Horst and at Frens, presumably of the early to mid-1560s,[120] may be relevant in this connection. Both of these, in any case, could well be the work of Johannssen's German associate, Laurentz von Brachum, and not by the Dutch architect from Arnhem himself.

The gable on Schloss Horst-im-Broiche, in the Ruhr district near Essen, is not extant but is known from a drawing (Fig. 57) made in 1842 before the demolition of the east wing. To judge from the drawing, the front of the gable was not really staged. Rather, the plain near-

strapwork elements of the surface decoration were combined—as a bit later at Frens (Fig. 58), which lies farther south, in the Rhineland west of Cologne—into a sort of all-over grid consisting of curved forms linked by horizontals and verticals. Though the outline of the gable at Horst was in a sense scalloped, this resulted from the detailing of the bandwork at the edges. At Horst there was really no scrolling at all, while at Frens, even though there are some curving elements in the outline, the scalloping is rather flaccid and unemphatic, at least by Vredeman's new standards of the 1560s.

The spirit is that of the Netherlander's published gable designs, but there seems not to have been any direct filiation. Uncertainty as to the date of the Horst gable, however, makes an indirect connection just possible chronologically. Neither in the Dutch development of the scrolled gable nor in the parallel German story do these gables—that at Horst probably well known to contemporaries, if not the more modest example at Frens—have an important place. But whoever designed that at Horst was employing all-over bandwork at least as early on a gable, indeed possibly a year or so earlier, as Vredeman in the gable designs in his *Architectura* of 1563.

Still of this same decade are two more notable facades in Gdańsk by the Saxon architect Johann Kramer, that at Długa 35 (Fig. 59) and the so-called English or Angel House at Chlebnicka 16. The former, called the Lion's Castle, carries the date 1569.[121] It has big Dutch windows on all four storeys separated by pilasters. Above the fourth storey the gable has only one stage. This is richly decorated, but the pediment that caps it is broad and plain. The gable of the English House has not been restored since World War II. Built in 1570,[122] that gable is less typically Dutch than the ones on the Zielona Brama that Kramer had completed some years earlier, probably following the designs of the Amsterdamer Regnier (Fig. 54). But both the first and the second stages here were flanked by bold and heavily carved scrolls, while the third stage had smaller scrolls beneath an equally vigorous pedimental termination. Despite the greater height of the facade below, the proportions of the three stages are closer to German gables of this date, such as the one on the Johann Rike house at Hameln[123] on the Weser in Westphalia, than to anything thus far erected in Holland, much less Brabant or Flanders. They cannot be so closely matched in Saxony, however, whence Johann Kramer came to Gdańsk.

The development of the scrolled gable does not seem to have proceeded as consistently and rapidly in the Netherlands as in Germany, most particularly in the Weser region there. The facade of the Boterhal of the *Sint-Jansgasthuis* (St. John's hospice) in the Kerkplein at Hoorn (Fig. 60), a port on the IJsselmeer in Noord Holland, is the most elaborate that survives in the Netherlands from the sixteenth century. This is dated 1563. For all its broad pedimented window groups, however, so unlike the proto-Academic single windows with pediments in Erfurt (Fig. 56), and the profusion of sculptural decoration, the gable is still a stepped one. Each of the relatively tall steps forms a stage and is surmounted by an entablature that repeats the one crowning the main storey below. The carved decoration that flanks all three stages does approach a scrolled outline; yet, as on the contemporary Raadhuis in Antwerp, that outline is actually made up of figural elements. It is interesting to note, as regards the late use of boldly scrolled gables in this town, that the two on the front of the *Raadhuis* (Fig. 94) date from 1613 and the central one on the *Doelen* from 1615.

A very much larger structure than either of these at Hoorn—so large in intention that it was never completed—is the *Kanselarij* (chancery) in Leeuwarden, capital of the province of Friesland (Fig. 61), built 1566–71. Much of the detailing on this is actually still of medieval character, and the articulation of the walls as a whole follows Netherlandish Late Gothic models. Flattened semi-elliptical arches cap windows subdivided by molded stone mullions and transoms in a series of identical bays. Even more Gothic in aspect is the single tall gable that crowns the pair of bays—evidently meant to be the central ones—above the main entrance. The relief treatment of the surface of this gable, though carried out with elements of the orders, is so structured vertically that the pilasters have almost the look of flattened buttresses. Moreover, the seven statues on the narrow steps of the gable still suggest medieval finials; while the small round arches in the two bays and the lunettes above them, the Renaissance elements, are barely noticeable. In any case, these recall work of a generation earlier; and nothing in the way of scrolled or bandwork ornament indicates familiarity with Vredeman's published designs of the 1560s as would, indeed, be unlikely so early.

So also the already mentioned speeltoren at Edam in the province of Noord Holland, which was carried upward in 1568–69 to hold the bells cast by P. v. d. Gheiyn in Mechelen in 1561, is actually more Gothic looking than Dirksen's grander one of a decade earlier in Gdańsk. The tall brick shaft below the crown is a survival of the O. l. Vrouw-Kerk of the fifteenth century and the detailing of the octagonal belfry stage in sandstone is as hybrid and belated as that on the gable of the Hoorn Kanselarij.

Along with the laggard acceptance of Renaissance and Northern Mannerist design in Dutch, particularly northern Dutch, architecture in the 1560s, the diaspora from Catholic Brabant south of the Schelde continued, especially in the next decade. In 1574–76[124] the presumably Protestant builder-architect Laurens I van Steenwinckel built the Rathaus in Emden (Fig. 62), the principal port in German Ostfriesland across the Eems from the Dutch province of Groningen. Whether or not Steenwinckel had actually worked a decade earlier in Antwerp on the Raadhuis, he certainly had that in mind, though the structure he executed was smaller and considerably more simply detailed. Unlike the front of the Leeuwarden Kanselarij (Fig. 61), however, there was little here to suggest Gothic inheritance. The main roof was hipped and the two-stage gable above the asymmetrically placed entrance had a pilaster order on both stages. Moreover, there was rich scrolled carving beside the upper stage as well as obelisks at that level and flanking the terminal pediment above.

In Denmark in the 1570s[125] three Netherlanders were employed by Frederik II on the Kronborg Slot at Helsingør, on the Sond at the entrance to the Baltic, to replace a fifteenth-century castle. Whence precisely came Hans van Paeschen (Paaske or Pasche) who began the work in 1574 is not clear, but Anthonis van Opbergen (1543–1611), who took charge in 1577, was from Mechelen; with him was associated as *underbygmester* (assistant chief architect), at least by the early 1580s, Hans I van Steenwinckel. Born in Antwerp, the young Hans had assisted his father Laurens I earlier at Emden. Later he succeeded Opbergen in 1585 as *oberbygmester* at Kronborg when Opbergen moved on to Gdańsk. Hans I van Steenwinckel[126] is documented as having provided also the design of the house Uraniborg and the observatory he built over the years 1576–89[127] for the great Danish astronomer, Tycho Brahe, on the island of Hveen in the Sond.

The four wings of the quadrangular Kronborg Slot, as cased in stone by Opbergen and Steenwinckel, have end gables and also a profusion of gabled dormers (Fig. 63) added later. These vary somewhat in design, but they are all staged and also flanked by bold scrolls and sharp obelisks. Unhappily, Kronborg castle burned in 1629, but from 1631 on it was restored by Christian IV.[128] He employed Hans II van Steenwinckel (1587–1639); but this architect, trained in Holland under Lieven de Key, for the most part followed quite closely what Opbergen and his own father had done. The mixture of elements belonging to the 1570s and 1580s with later renewals and additions is confusing historically. For example, the octagonal corner tower dominating the whole Slot is of the early 1580s, but the big scrolled gable of the chapel beside it is in its present form of the period after the fire in the seventeenth century and the work, therefore, like the score or more gabled stone dormers above the eaves, of the younger Steenwinckel. The tallest feature, the Trumpeters' Tower, resembling a Dutch speeltoren in its present form, is dated 1777, but it was closely modeled on the one Hans II built in the 1630s.

Because of the use of masonry throughout—a real luxury in Denmark not continued elsewhere by Christian IV—and perhaps because of modification of the design of some of the large gables when restored or rebuilt after the 1629 fire, the Kronborg Slot looks today, like Swedish castles of the period, more Germanic than Netherlandish. But Opbergen's origin became more obvious in what he built afterward in Gdańsk, since that is all of brick. In Holland the use of brick, though with increasing amounts of dressing in stone, has necessarily continued, even to some extent down to the present, though not in most of Belgium.

GABLES OF THE 1570S

The *Kasteel Cannenburg*, just outside Vaassen in Gelderland, is difficult to date as regards the tower that projects on the front. Although the core of the structure is medieval and there was much remodeling in the eighteenth century, the architectural decoration on the tower is certainly of the sixteenth century and possibly, at least, of the early 1570s. A chimneypiece inside carries the date 1577, a year after the death of the wife of the owner, Hendrick van Isendom. This may indicate the termination of his work on the Kasteel. As he lived on until 1594, however, there were for all its distinctly early appearance still many years within which he might have carried on the work.

There is no real gable at Cannenburg, but stone elements set in the brick facade provide the outline of a three-stage one (Fig. 64). This is flanked in the upper portion of the first and second stages by long narrow scrolls tightly spiraled at their bottom ends. The delicacy of scale of this stonework on the tower and of the paneled pilasters on the two storeys of the main wall, as well as the fluting on the crowning lunette, recall the detailing of the facade of 1549 on the house at Markt 11 in Culemborg (Fig. 33). That suggests a midcentury date rather than one in the last quarter, but is not conclusive. The work may well have been very retardataire.

Whatever the date of the Cannenburg decorations, it was in the 1570s that the Renaissance, or post-medieval, decorated gable, introduced some fifty years earlier on the Palais de Savoie, came to maturity in the Netherlands both northern and southern in Northern Mannerist guise. Specific influence from Vredeman—most particularly from his designs of 1563, though somewhat reinforced by his later publications—is less obvious than a new assurance in the combination of scrolled elements of outline related to strapwork on the wall surface; yet simpler gable patterns, especially stepped ones, were still in use, as has already been noted, which would be true well into the next century.

The finest extant example in Holland of a gable of the 1570s is the one over the front of the *De drie Haringen*, as it is called, a house that is now part of the Stedelijk Museum of Deventer in the province of Overijsel (Fig. 65). This is dated 1575. The ground storey and mezzanine seem to have been refaced in the eighteenth century, however; only the upper two storeys and the gables front and back are of the sixteenth century. On the rear the walls are without architectural elaboration except for the entablatures above the first and second stages of the gable. But the ends of these break the sloping sides much as at Huis Twickel (Fig. 39). The two stunted obelisks at the sides above the second stage and the terminal pediment on this gable hardly prepare one for the elaboration of the one over the front.

On the front facade of De drie Haringen both the two upper storeys and the first two stages of the gable are articulated vertically by a pilaster order and horizontally both by entablatures—richer versions of those on the rear—and by inset bands of stone. Stone blocks also provide the keystones and haunches of the bearing arches over the wood-mullioned windows. All these interpolated elements of stone have textured surfaces, somewhere between vermiculation and chip-carving in character, as is at least suggested in various of Vredeman's designs. Shortly this was introduced even more profusely on the walls, pilaster order, and arch on the inner side of the *Oosterpoort* at Hoorn by Joost Jann Bihamer, which carries the date 1578, although that gate has no gable above.

The boldly scrolled outline of the front gable on De drie Haringen is surprisingly like that of the gables completed, presumably by Hans Knotz, nearly forty years earlier on the north wing of Ottheinrich von der Pfalz's Schloss at Neuburg-a.-d.-Donau (Fig. 16). The first stage at Deventer has convex C-scrolls along the edges that are tightly spiraled at the lower ends and surmounted by short straight elements. The next stage has concave C-scrolls of which the spiraled lower ends are capped by heraldic beasts. The third has both small concave C-scrolls at its base and then a combination of convex scrolls and verticals like the bottom stage. This is crowned with a slightly enriched version of the pediment on the rear gable. On the wall surface throughout this facade the horizontal stone banding is textured, as are the alternating stone voussoirs in the bearing arches and around the circular feature in the top stage. That is connected at the cardinal points with the vertical elements at the sides, the entablature above, and the window arch below by additional textured bands, much as on the top stage of Regnier's gables of the previous decade on the Zielona Brama in Gdańsk (Fig. 54).

In Flanders the gables of the Wenemaerhospital in Gent (Fig. 49), of the previous decade, though more boldly scrolled in outline, lack S-curves altogether. They therefore seem rather simplified in design and also, indeed, somewhat provincial in execution compared with the Dutch example in Deventer (Fig. 65). Not surprisingly the two gables are more like the single ones on such other Gent facades as were described earlier (Figs. 26, 49). Very likely, however, scrolled gables at least as elaborate as that in Deventer once topped some of the facades in the Groote Markt in Antwerp before the fire of 1576.

Of Antwerp gables surviving the fire—not to speak of the damage done in two twentieth-century wars—neither that of the early 1540s over the Wewershuis (Fig. 24) on the south side nor the so much more monumental one of the Raadhuis (Fig. 46), on the west, of twenty years later can properly be described as scrolled. But, on the north side, one gabled facade of the post-fire years, 1579-82,[129] is extant which is much grander than any in Gent. The facade is that of the *Oude Voetbooggildehuis* (archers' guildhouse) as restored after the last war (Fig. 66). Its four storeys are so similar to those of the Wewershuis it may actually represent the "renewal" of a pre-fire design of 1560 or even earlier. The fronts of the guildhouses to the right were rebuilt in Brabantine Late Gothic after the last war. They suggest, all the same, to what extent this particular sixteenth-century one, though so late in date, represented still a translation into Renaissance—or more usually, as in this case, Northern Mannerist—terms of an inherited sort of gridded fenestration. In the south such fenestration long continued to be common in contrast to the very broad individual windows increasingly used in Holland from the mid-century on. But the gridding has no arches in the way of the earlier and later facades in Gent (Fig. 26).

The three central bays of the first stage of the archers' gable repeat the articulated grid of the facades below and there is a fourth single window, slightly smaller in size, at the center of the second stage. Between the stages the entablatures of the storeys below are also repeated, but in much more vigorous relief. So also the scroll elements at the sides of the first stage, more similar in general design to those on De drie Haringen (Fig. 65) than to those in Gent, are large in scale and flat in what may be considered the Vredeman manner. Instead of the tight spirals at the base of this stage on the Deventer facade, the scrolls in Antwerp enclose wreathed rondels carved with the longbows of the archers. These resemble a little the rondels carved with heads on De Graven van Vlaanderen in Gent.

The next stage on the facade of the archers' guildhouse in Antwerp has again broad flat bands at the sides, here S-scrolled; while the terminal one is similar to that at Deventer, but narrower and unpedimented. The liveliness of the outline against the sky is much enhanced by the pairs of slim spiky obelisks flanking the scrolls and, above all, by the statue of the guild's patron, St. George, on a rearing horse, which provides the crowning feature. English guilds, or City Companies as they are called in London, seem not yet to have been so grandly housed; at least nothing comparable to the Antwerp examples survives from this period.

Although so-called Dutch gables—as will be discussed later in chapter XI—were commonly used in London over houses, especially along Holborn, in the second quarter of the seventeenth century in the time of Charles I and even a good deal earlier, scrolled gables were rare in Elizabeth I's time. In large part this was because of the continuance of the low and often invisible roofs in general use under the Tudors. Moreover, from at least the designing of Somerset House under Edward VI in the 1540s, Italian influence reinforced the local tradition, and country houses of any pretension were likely to be crowned with Italianate balustrades. There are, however, two major exceptions that are very well known.[130] The design of the openwork scrolled elements imitating gables that top the towers at Wollaton Hall in Nottinghamshire (Fig. 67) was definitely borrowed by the builder-architect Robert Smythson (?1536–1614) from Vredeman's plates, as was other ornament used there on the screen of the hall. Wollaton was begun at the end of the decade around 1580 and completed by 1588.[131]

The building of Kirby Hall in Northamptonshire started ten years earlier; but the construction, interrupted in 1575, dragged on, probably even into the early 1580s. The rear wing with its elaborate scrolled gables decorated all over with strapwork ornament of an up-to-date Northern Mannerist sort (Figs. 68, 69) must be, at the earliest, of the mid to late 1570s.[132] These gables differ markedly from the more formal design of the court facades. In them, by contrast, Pevsner sees a reflection of the chateau of Saint Maur in France, especially in the use of a giant order of pilasters. The designer, or perhaps the executant hand, may have been Netherlandish, but the ornament could just as well have been borrowed from Vredeman's plates by an English craftsman, perhaps one who had actually been trained in Antwerp like the German Jürgen Crossmann of Lemgo in Westphalia at this time. The Kirby gables certainly fit better with continental examples of the 1570s than with other English work of the middle years of Elizabeth I's reign. But the pace of development on the continent was changing now. In the northern Netherlands this was because of increasing prosperity; in the south, to relative independence of Spanish rule, at least in the early 1580s as regards Antwerp.

THE BOLLAERTSKAMER IN GENT

Contrasting with the dilute Italianism of Smythson's Elizabethan mansions of the 1580s and 1590s, Wollaton or Hardwick, is the facade of the Bollaertskamer in Gent (Fig. 70).[133] This rose in 1580–82 in the Hoogpoort at the far end of the long front of the Raadhuis as built by Rombout Keldermans and Domien de Waghemaekere in 1518–35. Still greater is the difference from the lush Brabantine Late Gothic of that earlier work, the masterpiece of its architects. Except for the stone mullions and transoms of the windows and the dormers, which once rose over the second and fourth bays, this three-storeyed composition of paired and engaged columns, all executed in cut stone, might well be taken for Italian work of the mid-sixteenth century, or at least that of some Italian working abroad. Even the banding of the Doric order seems no more than an echo of Italian Mannerism. Indeed, the only northern note in the surviving facade is the profuse use of chip-carving for the podia of the lowest order and for those bands. This relatively new decorative treatment, not employed in any profusion even in the northern Netherlands before the previous decade, seems here merely an alternative to such conventionally Italianate enrichment as rustication or vermiculation often used in these years all over Europe.

Above the entablature of the Corinthian order of the top storey, which lines up with the cornice of the earlier facade to the left, a sixteenth-century watercolor by Lieven van der Scheiden (Fig. 71) indicates that there were originally stone dormers not only over two bays of the early structure but also, as just mentioned, over two of the bays of the newer Bollaertskamer. These seem to have been nearly as Italianate in their design as the facade below. Each included a good-sized window under an arch. This arch, with its molded imposts and its keystone, was enframed either by pilasters or by engaged columns, and there was a full entablature above. No scrolls flanked this stage of the gablets. Atop the entablature, however, the next stage was not, as seems at first glance, a segmental pediment but was made up of two flattened S-scrolls. These scrolls were linked by a short rectangular element that rose to a plain pedimental crown.

A good deal of information survives as to the stonemasons and other craftsmen involved in the construction of the Bollaertskamer. Yet this is not altogether satisfying as to who in particular was responsible for the advanced design, which is much more Academic than Cornelis Floris's of twenty years before for the Antwerp Raadhuis. Credit is usually given to the city architect Joos Rooman[134] rather than to Frans van de Kethulle, lord of Ryhove, who supervised the work for the authorities, or to the prominent citizen, Jan Bollaert, who laid the cornerstone and whose name has remained attached to the work. The names of a carpenter, Niclaeys vander Burcht; a metalworker, Pieter de Scheppere; and several stone-masons, Franchois vande Waele, Sebastiaen van den Linden, Bonnifaes Pollet, and Joos Coen, are known; but the contracts with these last required that they follow the *patroon* of Rooman. It is unlikely, in any case, that they were innovating proto-Academics, so to put it, as Rooman may have been. Rooman, however, could have consulted other master builders, though it is hard to name Netherlanders other than Sebastiaan van Noyen, as represented by his long-lost work of thirty years before for Cardinal Granvella in Brussels, sufficiently instructed in the Academic discipline of sixteenth-century Italy to have assisted. Not many of this date even in France would have been capable of designing and supervising the execution of the facade in Gent. Certainly nothing that survives from this decade in Holland is at all comparable, except for the profuse use of chip-carving, which was well under way there by the 1570s. Rather, in these years, typically Northern Mannerist production, particularly scrolled gables, increased in quantity, to judge at least from what is extant.

DUTCH GABLES OF THE 1580S AND EARLY 1590S

According to H. E. van Gelder,[135] "shortly after 1580 a revival of monumental architecture took place" in Holland; but he does not offer examples of extant work earlier than the 1590s or even after 1600. There are relevant works that are earlier, however. At Kalverstraat 92 in Amsterdam the surviving portal of the Burgerweeshuis carries the date 1581. Monumental in scale, this has a profusion of chip-carving on the imposts and the voussoirs, but no gable. All the same, that fragment of a semi-public building in Amsterdam of the early 1580s is quite overshadowed by the contemporary *Waag* at Alkmaar (Fig. 72). This was erected by the civic authorities of a town in Noord Holland, then of considerable im-portance, that had survived a Spanish siege in 1573. The core of the structure had been the chapel of the H. Geesthuis; but the eastern arm, entirely rebuilt in 1582, is topped by the most ornate gable yet erected in the Netherlands, except for that of the Antwerp Raadhuis.

The ground storey of the Alkmaar Waag has open archways between brick and stone piers, but the arcade and also the mezzanine above are largely masked today by the marquee of the market. The first storey, with three broad bays on the end and two on either side, is of brick; but the pilaster order is more heavily banded in stone than on such comparable facades as that of the Zielona Brama in Gdańsk of the 1560s (Fig. 54) or De drie Haringen in Deventer of the 1570s (Fig. 65), if not the Nieuwe Oosterpoort in Haarlem. The surface of the first stage between the pilasters is loaded with sculpture as are the roughly scroll-shaped elements at its sides. These last were presumably intended to rival the similar elaboration at the sides of the upper stages of the front gable on the Antwerp Raadhuis (Fig. 46). The next stage is flanked by obelisks set beyond the scrolling sculpture at the sides. Above that, urns accompany the simpler and more vigorous S-scrolls of the top stage. This stage, as so often, concluded in a pediment, here carrying a ball-topped element. The crossing tower was added later in 1597–99.

Very different is the Sint Joris-doelen (Fig. 73) at Middelburg in Zeeland, which carries the date 1582. Like the Raadhuis the Keldermans, Anthonis I and Rombout, built in the early decades of the century there, the front of this is all of stone, but its simplicity contrasts with the extreme elaboration of the earlier structure. The two storeys have regularly spaced windows, exceptionally tall in their proportions and without framing in the masonry—except for tiny moldings on the lintels of the upper storey—around the flush lights with their wooden mullions and transoms. The only accented feature, and that very small and plain for the period, is the off-center portal with its banded imposts and voussoirs below a simple pediment.

The striking impression made by this modest facade at Middelburg is produced by the wide cross-gable, a post-war reconstruction replacing the original which was demolished in 1940. Perhaps the restorers simplified the design, omitting ornament. As seen today there are no architectural elements of detail except for the generous S-scrolls that flank the first and second stages and the plain pediment capped by the statue of the titular saint, George, on his rearing horse mounted atop a paneled block. Carving is restricted to the city's arms set high on the surface of the first stage of the gable and two further achievements over the central windows of the upper storey. The exceptional simplicity of the masonry work is balanced by the decorative numerals at this level giving the date and by the bold painted designs, so beautifully scaled to the whole facade, that the restorers have used on the wooden shutters opening from the lower lights of the windows.

A considerably more ambitious civic structure, and of the more characteristic brickwork with stone trim, was the *Rietdijksche Poort* of 1590[136] at Dordrecht. This city gate was de-molished in 1832, but the outer side is known from an eighteenth-century watercolor

(Frontispiece). It was a triple composition with a large arch in the center flanked by pilasters banded by flat rustication. This portal, all of stone, rose to the full height of the small houses beside the gate. The lower sections, more in scale with the houses, were of brick only sparsely banded in stone. All of stone, however, were the scrolled elements outlining the broad central gable and the much smaller ones that flanked it. The S-scrolls and C-scrolls of the outline were connected to the banded pattern of the faces of the gables. The pediment over the central gable was capped with a pediment on which a pair of (?) lions reposed on either side of an obelisk. In the first stage of the main gable a pair of windows were framed by banded pilasters and banded flat arches. Above was a single smaller window similarly framed.

In Middelburg, moreover, there is a facade, quite different from either the Sint Joris-doelen there or the Dordrecht gate. The house known as *In de Steenrotse* (Fig. 74) also carries the date 1590, together with a profusion of carved figural reliefs hardly to be matched in this period in the Netherlands north or south. But the designer who, as a stonemason, will also have been the executant, seems to have been Andries de Valkenaere, from the southern Netherlands, and the material is Gotland sandstone with no visible brickwork at all. The nearly total glazing of the lower storeys and the middle bays of the topmost one, with arches over all the wide openings below and over the axial one above, recalls the sixteenth-century guildhouse facades of Gent and Antwerp (Figs. 18, 19, 24, 66), particularly the tapered membering of the upper storeys, more than anything else that survives in the north.

The big C-scrolls flanking the top storey of In de Steenrotse encircle medallions. These contrast by their large scale and bold relief with the delicate figural reliefs below the window lights in the middle and top storeys. The terminal gable was destroyed, like that of the Sint Joris-doelen, in 1940 and the horizontal crowning cornice must be modern, if not the carved brackets and heads that support it.

Equally profusely decorated with carved stone, so that the brickwork of the walls is visible only in a few restricted passages, is a gable in Deventer inscribed with the date 1591 (Fig. 75). The three bays to the right of the entrance of the Penninckshuis at Brink 85 seem to be entirely the work of those who restored the structure in 1890, and the composition is clipped on the left by a later housefront. The flavor of the whole is more northern than that of In de Steenrotse. However, the statue-filled niches with their fluted heads under pediments—pointed in the main storey and in the upper portion of the gable, horned in the lowest stage—have an earlier, almost a *quattrocento*, look that contrasts with the characteristically Northern Mannerist detailing of the arched entrance below and of the bold scrolling above. Such retardation is not uncommon around 1590, nor is it extreme compared to that even of public buildings in smaller towns. What is exceptional here is not the stylistic ambiguity but the great variety of the elements in the nearly all-over carved decoration. The large scale of the heraldic lions immediately above the portal and that of the bandwork on the "frieze" that runs across between the storeys contrasts with the delicacy of the six figures in the niches, a delicacy echoed in that of their settings. Yet the result is more coherent than—as one might say—it has any right to be!

The tiny step-gabled *Raadhuis* of Oudewater, a small place in Zuid Holland between Gouda and Utrecht, dates from 1588, but was renewed in 1887, and the equally simple and retarded Waag there is of 1595, a little later. Also quite small, but more boldly bichromatic, is the 1591 gable of the *Sint Joris-doelen* in Haarlem. The stone banding on this facade has a very large scale that justifies the relative crudity of the scrolls at the sides and the little paired arches over the openings. A similar crudity must have characterized another small gable of this precise date, that on the corner of the *Raadhuis* at Purmerend which was set at right angles to the much plainer (and earlier?) stepped gable on the end. The banding in stone is restricted there, however, to a few flat string-courses in a nearly vernacular way.

The slightly later *Raadhuis* (Fig. 76) of 1591–94 at Franeker, between Leeuwarden and the IJsselmeer in Friesland, restored by P. J. H. Cuijpers in 1887, is more comparable in size to the Alkmaar Waag (Fig. 72). However, it is not so advanced in style or so heavily scaled either as that or the Dordrecht gate (Frontispiece), much less as richly decorated with inset reliefs as the house in Middelburg (Fig. 74). The designer was P. A. Ens, then a municipal officer. With its semi-elliptical banded arches and three very tall and steep-stepped gables, indeed, it is almost as retardataire as the Leeuwarden Kanselarij of twenty-five years before. All the same, it is considerably more remote in its late-sixteenth-century vernacular way from the near-Gothic of Leeuwarden (Fig. 61). The crowning feature, as long before on the Zierikzee Raadhuis (Fig. 36), is a staged lantern; but this is rivaled in Holland at this date only by the speeltoren at Monnikendam of 1591. The latter tops an early-sixteenth-century square brick tower which was always free-standing and associated neither with a church nor with a town hall.

The employment of Netherlanders was by the 1590s an old story in Gdańsk, beginning with Daniel Dirksen's design of 1559 for what is still the tallest Dutch speeltoren of the sixteenth century. That is grander even than the one which survives in Monnikendam of a generation later, if not the Amsterdam towers of the next period by Hendrick de Keyser. In the 1570s and 1580s these aliens included the Van den Blockes, first Egidius and then Willem, who had earlier been active at Königsberg in East Prussia in 1576. Whether they had come from Antwerp or from Holland is not clear nor, perhaps, at this point important. In 1592 even Vredeman himself appeared on the scene, but he worked here as a painter. The most productive architect-builder—which Vredeman was not—was Anthonis van Opbergen, by then a man of fifty. When his work for Frederik II of Denmark was winding to a close and

Hans I van Steenwinckel took over at Kronborg in 1585, he came to Gdańsk and built in 1586–95 the Town Hall in the Old Town; a year or so later he rebuilt the *Więzienna* (prison) tower beside the Wyzynna gate, which was then being erected by Johann Kramer in association with Willem Van den Blocke.[137] In 1592 he became city architect, but the construction of his major monument in Gdańsk, the Great Arsenal, lay well ahead in the next decade.

Opbergen's crowning gable over the front portion of the Gdańsk prison tower (Fig. 77) is a richer example of what may be called the Vredeman mode than any of those he had built earlier at Helsingør (Fig. 63). However, it is not impossible—though rather unlikely— that some of the bigger Kronborg gables were simplified by Hans II van Steenwinckel after the fire of 1629 when he added the small gabled dormers and, in fact, is known to have modified the big gable over the outer end of the chapel. The principal stage of Opbergen's gable at Gdańsk is flanked by lower elements decorated with blind arches. From the extradoses of these arches obelisks rise and their bases, carved with human heads, are linked to the entablature of the tall central bay by C-scrolls. The vertical elements of the order here, though provided with Ionic capitals, are tapered herms. These are banded, as is most of the other stonework, by chip-carved blocks. The terminal stage, below a plain pediment, is accompanied by another pair of obelisks and, at the bottom, by heavy convex C-scrolls. On the face an oculus is linked to the framing, up and down and right and left, by stone bands in the familiar way as already here in Gdańsk on the gables of the Zielona Brama twenty years before (Fig. 54).

VII   Academic Reaction in Holland and Flanders

OPBERGEN'S almost excessive elaboration of the stone trim on the gable of his brick-built Wiezienna tower in the Baltic port at the mouth of the Vistula was soon rivaled in the northern Netherlands on the long facade, all of stone, of the Leiden Raadhuis. This fronts on the Breestraat, the main street of that Dutch university town. Lying at the mouth of the Waal, Leiden was still a viable port and perhaps as prosperous as Gdańsk—this, at least, the town hall certainly suggests. For the central three-stage gable of the Leiden Raadhuis and the facade below it an elevation of 1594 (Fig. 78) by Lieven de Key (c. 1560–1627)[138] survives. This shows bold scrolling on the gable between pairs of obelisks and a richly carved edicule topped by a pediment above. There is, however, no strapwork decoration at all, which is rather exceptional for the late date.

The executed gable (Fig. 79) in Leiden differs considerably. That difference is usually explained by the fact that the builder-architect, Lüder von Bentheim (c. 1550–1612/13), from the port city of Bremen near the mouth of the Weser, provided the stone used on the facade as a more monumental substitute for Dutch brick. This is Bückeburg sandstone from the quarries Bentheim controlled at Obernkirchen, near Minden in Westphalia. It is thought he may also have determined, at least partially, the character of its working. The result is certainly more typical of Northern Mannerist design than de Key's project. It is not, however, much like the facade on the Rathaus in Bremen, for which Bentheim was probably to some considerable degree responsible in the following decade.[139]

As on Opbergen's Gdańsk tower, terms are substituted for pilasters on the front of the Leiden Raadhuis in the bottom stage of the central gable above the entrance. Even more notable, by contrast to the project, is the strapwork decoration on the surface of the side bays of this stage and on the central bay of the second stage. Chip-carved banding is quite lacking, though by this time it was even more ubiquitous in the Weser valley region of Germany, whence came Lüder, than in Holland. The treatment of the two gabled dormers flanking the central gable is similar, but with caryatid herms instead of architectonic terms in the lower stage.

Because of the light-colored imported stone with which it is faced and the length of the front—extended to the east in 1604, then to the west in 1662 and 1735, and restored after a fire of 1929 more symmetrically, when the tower of 1599 to the rear was also rebuilt—this is the most impressive of Dutch town halls, contrasting in its horizontal extension and its Northern Mannerist detailing with the more princely Raadhuis of a generation before in metropolitan Antwerp. Whether Lieven de Key deserves most of the credit or should share it with Lüder von Bentheim remains uncertain.

Two other conspicuous public structures in the northern Netherlands, one known fairly definitely to be by Lieven de Key and the other only dubiously attributed to him, soon followed. The *Waag* in Haarlem, like Leiden then a large city rivaling Amsterdam, is the more important historically, though not as large as the *Gemeenlandshuis van Rijnland* in Leiden. But the latter, as the less advanced, may better be discussed first, both as executed in 1597–98 and as seen in a partial elevation, probably one actually drawn in 1597 by Lieven de Key (Fig. 80). Three bays, evidently intended to be the ones in the center, are indicated on the elevational drawing as of stone, with quoins at the corners and two entablatures. Though the lower entablature is not directly associated with the short Doric half-columns of the main arched portal, it does have Doric metopes. The pulvinated frieze of the upper entablature relates similarly to the Ionic volutes at the ends of the subsidiary entablatures topping the mullioned and transomed windows of the upper storey. Above the corners of the slight central projection banded obelisks rise, and between them the very tall lower stage of the gable is edged with multi-scrolled membering extending inward as strapwork. Two arched windows between Ionic pilasters occupy most of the central bay, with more scrolling strapwork above them. The terminal stage has an empty niche flanked at the base by bold scrolls and by strange elongated urn finials.

The side bays of the facade of the Rijnlandshuis were to be of brick, with stone quoins and strapwork scrolling only on the second stage of the gables. A much simplified version of that finish was used by the restorers in 1882 on these side gables which they reduced in size to gabled dormers. But the center gable, as originally built or as restored, is of a retardataire stepped pattern consonant with the almost vernacular treatment of the stone-banded brick walls of the facade below (Fig. 81).

In the miniscule geography of Holland, Haarlem is a bare twenty-five miles or so from Leiden, and Lieven de Key worked in both. But the Haarlem Waag, built in the same years near the end of the century as the Leiden Raadhuis and the Rijnlandshuis, is very different. In Holland this is the earliest—even though already nearly mature—example of a type of design that would within two decades be internationally accepted as a new canon in much of northern Europe, one already foreshadowed in the south by the Bollaertskamer in Gent of the 1580s (Figs. 70, 71). Loosely called Academic here rather than merely anti-Mannerist, this sort of design eventually brought Northern Mannerism to a belated end in the 1620s, at least as regards public buildings and work done for sophisticated private clients.

In 1596 two Haarlem painters, Willem Thybaut (c. 1524-c. 1598)[140] and Cornelis Cornelisz. (1562-1638), trained in France and in Antwerp,[141] were paid for providing three plans for the Waag. However, since de Key, who was the leading Dutch professional of the day, had been city architect of Haarlem since 1593, it has been assumed by some writers that he was really responsible for the Waag as executed in 1597-98 (Fig. 82). In support of this attribution was a balustrade that once ran all the way around above the cornice. This was evidently very like the one on the Leiden Raadhuis (Fig. 79), not to speak of that projected for the Rijnlandshuis (Fig. 81). Counting heavily against this attribution, right here in Haarlem is the totally opposed Northern Mannerist character of de Key's *Vleeshal* (meat market) of 1602-3 in the marketplace (Figs. 85, 86), which will be described shortly.

The use of stone throughout the Haarlem Waag—as on the Bollaertskamer in the south and on the Leiden Raadhuis, as well as de Key's proposal for the central bays of the Rijnlandshuis in Holland—rather than the more usual Netherlandish mixture of brick and stone, for the Rijnlandshuis as executed and the Vleeshal, might explain in part the severity of the composition. Moreover, the broad arched portals of the two Haarlem buildings with their banded rustication are very similar. On the other hand, except for the stone mullions and transoms, what might even this early be called—in an English term—the Jonesian window-frames of the principal storey of the Waag, with their vertical Italian proportions and alternately pointed and segmental pediments of a High Renaissance sort, have nothing in common with those of the Vleeshal. Moreover, the bold horizontal cornice that crowns the walls of the Waag, once topped with the balustrade that partially masked the roof, contrasts even more strikingly with the tall stepped gables over the ends of the latter (Fig. 85) and the dormers along the side (Fig. 86). Certainly little else survives in northern Europe after the Bollaertskamer in Gent (Figs. 70, 71) from these later years of the sixteenth century so premonitory as the facades of the Waag of the rather general turn toward the Academic that ensued some fifteen years or so later at several different centers in northern Europe which will be touched on as regards Holland in chapter VII.

Among conspicuous new works in the southern Netherlands, only the very considerable though rather uninteresting extension of the Raadhuis at Gent in Flanders (Fig. 83), all of stone but very inferior to the Bollaertskamer around the corner in execution, is relevant at this point. Designed and begun as early as 1595 by Loys Heindrickx, it was contemporary with the building of the Haarlem Waag; it was not completed by Arent van Loo and the Plumions, Pieter and Lieven, however, for some twenty-five years.[142] During those years even more truly Academic design was making an appearance in other regions of northern Europe; moreover, work by Rubens and by his friend Wencelas Coebergher that may almost be considered early Baroque was underway nearby in Brabant.

On this long structure in Gent it is the almost total disappearance—because of the crumbling of the stone—of the scrolls on the dormers above the long side and the end, as also the contrast of the regular rows of tall oblong windows of the new section, separated by plain pilaster orders only, with the lush Brabantine Late Gothic of the contiguous facades (Fig. 6) de Waghemaekere and Keldermans had erected nearly a hundred years earlier, that make so striking the changed character of the later additions, beginning already, indeed, with the Bollaertskamer of almost twenty years before (Figs. 70, 71). Yet the design of this later facade is hardly novel in the way either of that of the Haarlem Waag or, for that matter, of the Bollaertskamer here. It follows far more closely the Antwerp Raadhuis of 1561–65 than the latter, though without repeating the elaborate central frontispiece over the entrance or the hipped roof (Figs. 45, 46).

Leaving aside the Bollaertskamer of the early 1580s, mature design of the new formal sort actually appeared as soon in Switzerland as in Flanders. The main facade of the Rathaus in Luzern, begun by Anthony Isenmann in 1599,[143] only a few years after the Haarlem Waag and the later work in Gent, is provided with two regular rows of plain rusticated arches along the quay of the Reuss rather than with orders of columns and pilasters or edicular windows as at Gent or at Haarlem; but the result is at least as advanced in character as the Raadhuis extension, despite the late date of the completion of that, except for the heavy Swiss roof with which it is crowned.

So also in the larger structure in Flanders, it is the high gabled roofs that remain northern. The original design of the gabled dormers, one over the entrance bays—which are not in the center—and another near the left end, are barely to be made out in their present decrepit state, but can be seen more as they once were in old photographs (Fig. 83). They contrast with the more Academic pedimented dormers that once broke out of the high roof of the Bollaertskamer (Fig. 71). The two gables, better preserved than the others, that terminate the paired main roofs around the corner on the left are, surprisingly, not identical. The broader corresponds to four of the mullioned and transomed windows of the main walls and the other to two only. Both are in two stages, with scrolls flanking each of the stages. On the broader one niches are introduced on the inner sides of the scrolls, somewhat as Opbergen had done on the gable of the prison tower at Gdańsk well before this (Fig. 77). Though these seem to contradict the severe design of the main stories below, they can never have been, even when their terminal pediments survived, very bold examples of scrolled gables; neither, however, can they be considered even proto-Academic like the dormers on the Bollaertskamer (Fig. 71).

VIII   Gables in Holland of the Years around 1600

FROM THE VERY LAST YEARS of the sixteenth century and the first of the seventeenth a good many more gabled facades survive in the north than from any earlier period of similar length. The extremely rich facade dated 1599 of the tall and narrow *Raadhuis* of Brouwershaven in Zeeland, all of stone, was very heavily restored in 1890–91. The fussy detailing, whether or not a fair copy of the original work, may be considered provincial in this small port, which had been fortified only in 1590. The execution of the ashlar and, more particularly, of the carved decoration is only too obviously of that date. The gable that crowns the front has a lower stage shaped at the edges by rather coarse concave and convex scrolls, the latter repeated on the next stage below a terminal feature. That also has modest S-scrolls and is capped by a tall pedestal carrying a statue. Exceptional are the flower-filled urns mounted on projections at the upper edge of the lower stage and, again, on more solid supports at mid-height of the second stage.

A simpler but far more interesting gable than that at Brouwershaven tops the front of a modest house in Arnhem at Rijnstraat 41 (Fig. 84). The shopfront is, of course, modern; and the broad windows of the main story and the lowest stage of the gables with their elegant flat arches of rubbed brick are presumably of the late seventeenth or of the eighteenth century. But the staged gable, restored in 1913, has usually been loosely dated c. 1600 or "early 17th century."[144] The scrolled edges, all of thin stone members in convex and then in concave C-scrolls, are linked above and below the second stage by horizontal bands. Connected with those are other bands running out horizontally and vertically from band-framed oculi. Above the tall window in that second stage, also framed by banding decorated in delicate relief, the arch is capped with more intricate bandwork filling the upper portion of the top stage. Similar gables were used in Bocholt, on the German side of the present border, on the ends of the Rathaus there begun in 1618, and even later in Denmark in the 1620s at Copenhagen on the *Børsen* (exchange) and at Aalborg on the *Sten Hus* of Jens Bang (Figs. 107, 108, 109).

Lieven de Key's Haarlem Vleeshal of 1602–3, being a civic building, is naturally much larger and grander. Though its end gables carry no scrolling and that on the dormers on the long side is modest, they deserve a detailed description since these all remain distinctly Northern Mannerist in character with no evidence of proto-Academic chastening. The long front faces the Groote Kerk (Sint Bavo), but that on the northwest end is the principal one (Fig. 85). Above a half-basement and one main storey, the broad end gable rises in five stages separated by sharp string-courses. These are broken into a series of steps at the edges, two to a stage up to the fourth and one in the next. Obelisks above the lines of stone quoins on the corners top the lower step of the first stage and urns that of the third stage.

The face of the end gable on the Vleeshal has four windows in the first stage. Atop these, alternating voussoirs of stone radiate through the flat arches, as also over the two windows in the main storey below. The main arched portal between these, of which the resemblance to that of the earlier Waag (Fig. 82) has been noted already, has voussoirs all of stone and only plain horizontal rustication at the sides. Higher up, there are two windows capped by entablatures in the second stage of the gable and, over them in the next, a carved relief. The shallow fourth stage, however, has only a raised oblong block of stone for ornament. That is connected to the short stone bands that accent this stage in the same way similar ones do the lower ones. The terminal stage has an empty niche, presumably intended for a statue, and its crown is topped by a sort of urn-obelisk. The last two stages rise free above the actual roof behind, and so do those of the three gables on the long side over the roofs of the dormers they front. The east front is nearly identical up through the second stage of the gable. But in the third stage there are two oculi, from one of which a lifting beam projects. The topmost stages repeat those on the other end.

The gables of the dormers over the long side of the Haarlem Vleeshal (Fig. 86) rise above a main storey with windows like the ones on the ends. But these gables are not, as might be expected, merely reductions of those. On all of them, for example, short scrolls flank the windows in the lowest stage; but these modest scrolls all but disappear under the horizontals of the rusticated stone banding of the broad pilasters framing the windows. A pair of obelisks like those on the western corners also flanks this stage of the central gable. Above a complete entablature, the next stage is again elaborated with small scrolls and tiny sharp-pointed obelisks, while that in the center has a carved panel between a pair of slim pilasters. The topmost stages of the two side gables are quite similar to those of the end gables; but that in the center has a tall niche, once more flanked by pilasters, scrolls and obelisks, so that it is actually more elaborate than the corresponding top stage of the end gables.

There is no reflection at the Haarlem Vleeshal (Figs. 85, 86) of the severe style of the Waag (Fig. 82). Indeed, what is sometimes called Dutch Palladian would make no appearance for another score of years when Jakob van Campen, in 1625, designed the Koymanshuis in Amsterdam.

A small Northern Mannerist gable (Fig. 87) in Holland, of a few years later than those on the Vleeshal, is more exemplary. It is boldly scrolled and even carries the sort of flipped-up "horns" that are characteristic of this period in Hameln and the upper Weser valley in Germany. Dated 1605–6, this is over the *Kerkboog* in the market square of Nijmegen in Gelderland. At ground level two wide semi-elliptical arches lead to the Stevenskerkhof of the thirteenth-century Stevenskerk. These were built in 1542–45 by Claes de Waele and already display in their shape, as well as in their carved detail, evidence of Renaissance influence. That would be dominant here in Nijmegen a decade later in the design of the Raadhuis for which the stadbouwmeester Herman van Herengrave was responsible.

Quite different is the upper portion of the Kerkboog, dating from two generations later. In relief on the ashlar above the lower arches there are two panels with inscriptions that are framed in strapwork. In the center there is a lion with a shield, but that was presumably carved by Waele and of the earlier date. Then, in the upper storey, come three large windows subdivided by stone mullions and transoms, with wooden shutters opening from the lower lights. The wall here is of brick; but there are flush bands of stone and the Doric entablature, with its bold diamond bosses in the metopes, is all of stone also.

The gable of the Nijmegen Kerkboog has the usual combination of brick walling and carved stone detail. The successive scrolls of various sorts enlivening the outline are part of a rather coarse strapwork pattern which is accented by bosses at the intersections. This pattern covers the whole surface. The heavily molded terminal pediment above carries an obelisk on a pedestal.

The Kerkboog, the focal feature of the Nijmegen marketplace, contrasts with the much larger structure along the right side of the square, the *Waag*. Though built as late as 1612 as a weigh-house and meat market, it may be briefly noted at this point. The Waag can be considered a bit more "advanced," perhaps, than the Kerkboog, but as a result it seems rather dull and plodding. Doubtless that is partly because it was so heavily restored in 1886.

A less advanced but more impressive facade is the one of the *Stadsbushuis* of Amsterdam on the Singel (Fig. 88) which is attributed to Hendrick de Keyser. Dated 1606, this is a few years earlier than the Nijmegen Waag. On the ground storey here two wide, semi-elliptically arched doorways, plainly framed in stone, flank a severe main portal. That, however, may well be later than the wall above. In the main storeys, two rows of big windows under banded segmental arches are subdivided by mullions and transoms of white-painted wood and have wooden shutters for the lower lights. Irregular flush quoining in stone frames the plane of the walling in these two storeys. In the next storey the shuttered openings are smaller and there are narrow coupled arches over those in the center. The size of the outer openings at this level is, of necessity, reduced by the extremely heavy C- and S-scrolls that flank them.

The topmost stage of the facade, which was restored in 1919–21, has a very curious treatment. This suggests to what extent and how halfheartedly the vitality of late Northern Mannerism was now being modified by rising Academic influence. On the one hand, this stage terminates in a horizontal entablature rising from fluted pilaster strips; on the other, these last are truncated and without capitals or bases. They rise from carved bosses incorporated in a strapwork system that is linked with the upper C portion of the S-scrolls along the two edges. The C-scrolls are, in fact, repeated in reverse on either side of an oval feature in the center. That is framed by rather broader scrolling and incorporates the date 1606 carved on a plain tablet. Thus, at this level, the Bushuis facade has almost the air of being two, each of two bays, bound together by the horizontal entablature above. Such a linkage, carried out without relinquishing as here gabled terminations above, can be paralleled on the Great Arsenal that Opbergen, another Netherlander, had just completed in Gdańsk (Figs. 91, 92).

IX Netherlandish Northern Mannerism Abroad

THE FREDERIKSBORG SLOT OF CHRISTIAN IV OF DENMARK

WELL BEFORE THE END of the first decade of the seventeenth century the climactic Northern Mannerist monuments designed by Netherlanders had risen, not in present-day Holland or Belgium, but in Denmark and in Gdańsk, far to the north and to the east. The Danish king, Frederik II, had employed the Netherlander Anthonis van Opbergen on Slot Kronborg at Helsingør, it will be recalled, in the 1570s and 1580s. He also commissioned the tomb at Roskilde of Christian III in these years from Cornelis Floris, who executed it in Antwerp. He preferred living not at Slot Kronborg but at Hillerød, where he occupied a Late Gothic manor house, built toward 1550 for Herlaf Trolle, which he acquired in 1560. Of the work Frederik carried out at Hillerød over the twenty-eight years of his occupancy, only the *Badstuben* (bathhouse), begun as late as 1580,[145] probably by Johan (Hans) Floris, survives. This Floris, apparently no kin of Cornelis, had been working, since he came to Denmark from the Netherlands in 1568, with or under Opbergen on the Kronborg Slot and, before that, at Uraniborg for Tycho Brahe.

Frederik's successor, Christian IV, the brother of James I's queen, Anne of Denmark, began a small new house, *Sparepenge* (save money) probably in 1597, by which date he was already projecting a grander residence at Hillerød, but construction of the Frederiksborg Slot started only in 1602[146] and continued for some twenty years. The early designs for the Slot, probably dating from before 1600, have been attributed to Hans I van Steenwinckel. Hans I had worked earlier, like Johan Floris, with Opbergen at Slot Kronborg as *under-bygmester* (assistant master-builder) from 1582, after he had been employed—already with Floris—for four years at Uraniborg and, from 1585, as *overbygmester* at Kronborg. He and Christian are believed to have been influenced, particularly in the planning of the Slot at Hillerød, by the *Livre d'architecture* of 1559 by J. A. du Cerceau. A copy of this, known to have been in the Danish royal library in 1663, was probably acquired by Christian around 1600 if not earlier.

However that may be—and granting that the king himself was no Netherlander—many if not all the prominent features of the Frederiksborg Slot (Fig. 90) are unmistakably Netherlandish. The great tower that rises beside the chapel in the court is a sort of enlarged speeltoren and, indeed, held a big bell cast in 1614 and installed in 1615. By this time the king's wing on the left of the court, largely of the years 1602–6, was finished. The mason involved was Casper Boegendt, with whom the earlier of Christian IV's two contracts was dated December 16, 1601, and a later one for the chapel, 1608. The interiors of the king's wing were completed in 1611 before Boegendt's death the following year.

All the same, despite the similarity of the doors in the base of the stair towers at Frederiksborg to one Boegendt is known to have executed in 1584 at Kronborg, it does not seem probable that he was the responsible designer of the Slot as a whole. The great tower, which resembles particularly Hendrick de Keyser's tower of 1608–11 on the Amsterdam *Beurs* (exchange), has been attributed to Laurens II van Steenwinckel, son of Hans I and brother of Hans II; but for the realization, even on paper, of Christian's ideas, the two Hans van Steenwinckels seem more likely candidates. The elder had provided the design for the church at Slangerup near Hillerød in 1582. The younger is documented as having been responsible eventually for the terrace and the gallery of Frederiksborg. Also of his design are the stone oriels added on the king's wing, and some other things that were also carried out after 1614.

The Frederiksborg Slot has survived almost intact externally despite a fire in the nineteenth century which led to drastic internal restoration. From the tall towers in the forecourt and the main court to the gables on the ends of the wings and the gabled dormers along the roofs between, not to speak of the brick walls with sparse stone banding and much detail executed in stone, even the casual visitor can see that the look is Dutch (Fig. 90), though nothing of the period in Holland—much less still surviving in the southern Netherlands—is so large and so grand. The end gables, for all their great size, most resemble those on the house of about 1600 in Arnhem (Fig. 84) as do even more the smaller ones.

Many of the accessories at Frederiksborg were the work of Netherlanders also. The mason Boegendt, probably one of them, has been mentioned. He also definitely built the entrance gateway to the inner court. Later, the Barbican was begun in 1618, the year before Laurens died, by Hans II van Steenwinckel. Adriaen de Vries, Italian-trained but of Low Country birth, was paid 10,600 Rd for the Neptune fountain. This was commissioned by Christian in 1613 and carried out, first by Hans Brockman (doubtless also a Netherlander) down to his death in 1618, and then completed by the Dutch sculptor Johan Baptist Schyrmand in 1620–21, but according to a new scheme known to have been proposed by the king himself.[147] There will be considerably more to relate concerning Christian IV's building activity elsewhere in chapter XII.

THE GREAT ARSENAL IN GDAŃSK

The other culminating work of Netherlandish Northern Mannerist design, the Great Arsenal in Gdańsk (Figs. 91, 92), is neither so large nor was it so royally sponsored as the Frederiksborg Slot. It compares in the extravagance of its detailing, however, with such a princely work of the period as the grand Lutheran church at Bückeburg built a few years later, in 1610–15, by a German prince.[148] It is interesting to note at this point that the prince, Ernst von Schaumburg, had already commissioned Academic work by the Italian-Swiss Giovanni Maria Nosseni two years before. The client in Gdańsk was not the Swedish-born king of Poland, Zygmunt III, but the city authorities, who employed their own Mechelen-born city architect, not the king's Italian-Swiss Trevano. The Arsenal relates more in its moderate size and scale to the earlier city gate, the Zielona Brama (Fig. 54) of the 1560s—designed by the Amsterdamer Regnier, though carried out by Hans Kramer from Dresden—than to Christian IV's big Danish Slot (Fig. 90). The Arsenal was commissioned in 1602,[149] the same year the building of the Frederiksborg Slot began. Completed in 1605, long before Christian IV's castle, it was almost precisely contemporary with de Key's Haarlem Vleeshal of 1602–3 (Figs. 85, 86) as well as the Nijmegen Kerkboog (Fig. 87) and the Amsterdam Arsenal (Fig. 88), both dated in the early years after 1600.

Balancing the Zielona Brama, which extends across the east end of the principal Gdańsk square, the Długi Targ (Fig. 54), the Arsenal closes off the west end of the Piwna, the next street north of the Długa, the main street that continues westward the line of the square. At this end of the Długa itself the *Złota Brama* (golden gate) would soon rise also in 1612–14.[150] Both the Arsenal and the new gate were the work of Netherlanders: Abraham Van den Blocke, Willem's son, since 1596 a citizen of Gdańsk, for the latter; and Antonis van Opbergen for the former.

As will be remembered, Opbergen, born in 1532 in Mechelen, had been employed by

Frederik II of Denmark in the 1570s and early 1580s on the Kronborg Slot at Helsingør (Fig. 63). In 1585 he settled in Gdańsk and, in 1592, was appointed city architect, a post he retained until his death in 1611. His first considerable commission in Gdańsk, that for the Town Hall in the Old Town, was completed in 1595. Already, about 1587, he had rebuilt the portion described earlier (Fig. 77) of the Więzienna Tower that stands between Willem van den Blocke's contemporary *Wyżynna Brama* (high gate) and the Złota Brama.

Busy all along with the improvement of the Gdańsk fortifications, Opbergen was also responsible, at least reputedly, over the years 1598–1608[151] for the no longer extant north-east wing of a Schloss for the Margraves of Brandenburg. This is at Kostrzyn (Custrin) on the east bank of the Oder just north of Frankfurt. Rather more certainly of his design are the surviving corner turrets and gables of the top storey he added in 1602–3 to the fourteenth-century Town Hall at Torun (Thorn). Only his precisely contemporary Arsenal in Gdańsk[152] is in a class with the earlier work of which he had been in charge at Helsingør (Fig. 63).

At the head of the Piwna stands the broad facade of the Arsenal (Fig. 91). Its two octagonal stair towers, capped not with *welsche Hauben*—"Italian bonnets," as Germans of the period called them—but with pagoda-like multiple roofs that rise high above the facade, are each set one bay in from the ends and flank two gables in the center. These gables are linked to one another and to the towers by screen-walls crowned with bold C-scrolls and statues. One half of these unique features, turned inward, also surmounts each of the end bays beyond the towers, an extreme example of Mannerist syncopation. In the ground storey two arched portals, their frames banded with extremely bossy rustication, open into what is today a covered market devoid of architectural interest.

In the main storey of the Arsenal in Gdańsk a regular range of eight very tall windows with stone mullions and double transoms is interrupted by a pilaster-framed niche in which is set a statue, presumably of Bellona. In contrast to the high relief of the detailing of the portals, the wall at this level and, on the towers, in the next is flat with flush stone trim and stone-banded segmental bearing arches above the flat heads of the windows. The trim remains relatively simple in the top storey. Though the plane of the wall is continuous with that below, the top storey is actually also the lowest stage of the gables. At this level one tall window occupies the center of each gable and that window is flanked by smaller ones capped with stone bearing arches. Toward the top of the principal stage, where the two halves of the facade are linked by the big convex C-scrolls, bossy strapwork runs across below heavy cornices. These carry prominent obelisks on their projecting ends. The smaller top stage of each gable terminates in a segmental pediment from which what appears to be a bomb bursts upward. Below the pediments, oval oculi are connected by strapwork to three-dimensional sculpture that is confined by the flanking obelisks. The broad outer side of the building facing west (Fig. 92) is very similar in its elaborate detailing, but the flat plane of the facade, crowned by four identical gables, is not interrupted by stair-towers.

The Netherlandish bichromy of red brick with stone trim on the Arsenal recalls that of the Zielona Brama (Fig. 54). But Opbergen did not reflect the almost proto-Academic restraint characterizing some work in Gdańsk of the 1560s (Figs. 52, 54); there is rather, even for the early seventeenth century, an exceptional degree of animation of the whole wall surface. Resulting from variations in the projection of the decorative elements, this is only occasionally approached in facades of this period or later surviving in the Netherlands (Fig. 96).

X Countercurrents in Holland after 1610

AS IS OFTEN, perhaps usually, true in the history of architecture, it is not difficult to recognize the point at which the story of the Netherlandish scrolled gable began—at Mechelen, almost certainly in 1517. Despite recurrent overlapping, the approximate dates of initiation of the successive phases that followed, if not their duration, is also fairly clear and determinable. The situation is different as regards the conclusion of the main story in the early seventeenth century. The next major phase of Netherlandish architecture, of which such things as the Gent Bollaertskamer (Fig. 70) and the Haarlem Waag (Fig. 82) were already premonitory in the 1580s and 1590s, relates to that international reaction against Mannerism which is so evident in England in the work of Inigo Jones[153] and, in Germany, to a lesser degree in that of Elias Holl.[154]

The reaction was under-way in the second decade of the new century, from around 1609 in the case of Holl and from 1616–17—or just possibly 1613—for Jones. The Academic design of the Augsburg Rathaus by Holl, built 1615–24, or of the Whitehall Banquetting House by Jones of 1619–21 that soon followed, did not close off production of earlier character in Germany and England. All the same, the vitality of later Mannerist work seems to have diminished over most of northern Europe. Nor did new work illustrating

87

available Academic alternatives soon come to maturity—particularly not in Holland—even at the hands of trained professionals. For example, Hendrick de Keyser's *Waag* at Hoorn (Fig. 89), dated 1609, which will shortly be described in some detail, hardly yet rivals in its use of the new sort of design either Holl's or Jones's executed work of the next decade, nor did it initiate either in Holland or abroad any general stylistic modulation. Rather, in Holland it was Northern Mannerism—if to a lesser extent in Belgium—that still found striking expression in many elaborately gabled facades that are of considerable interest and quality despite their late date.

This account may well be concluded, if not finally terminated, with illustrations and descriptions of a certain number of these, down to the recognized opening of the Dutch Palladian phase in Holland with van Campen's Koymans house of 1625 in Amsterdam, and even in a few cases beyond the mid-1620s. The story does not end even in the third decade of the century. Indeed, what has long been considered Dutch influence may have continued in England down to the outbreak of the Civil War and even later. That matter has been saved for later discussion in chapter XI, a discussion including tentative conclusions differing from those of most—though not the latest—English writers on the architecture of the period.

The nearest Dutch rival, as a major late example of Northern Mannerism, to the Gdańsk Arsenal would be the *Raadhuis* at Bolsward in Friesland (Fig. 93) of the following decade. This was designed in 1613 by the mayor, a joiner named Jacob Gijsberts, and carried out over the next four years by the city's master-mason, Maerten Dominici. The exterior of their Town Hall, however, is very different because of the applied orders that play so great a part in the plastic elaboration of the upper walls and of the single central gable on the front. The prominence of the orders may seem to suggest that Gijsberts was trying to meet halfway the new standards of Academic design. However, those standards were not as yet fully adumbrated even by Holl—nor, it seems probable, by Jones—much less by any designer in the Netherlands other than whoever was responsible for the precocious Haarlem Waag.

It was in the year 1617, it will be recalled, when the Bolsward Raadhuis was completed, that Inigo Jones began to build the Queen's House at Greenwich that had been commissioned the previous year. Two years later than the initiation of the work at Bolsward and after a considerable period of gestation—perhaps as much as five years—while Schloss Willibaldsburg was rising at the behest of the ruling prince-bishop to his design outside the small city of Eichstätt in Swabia, Holl in 1615 started construction for the Rat of the vast Rathaus at Augsburg, the metropolis of the region. These two German landmarks of the Academic reaction against Northern Mannerism had—except for the much earlier Bollaertskamer in Gent in the south (Fig. 70) and the Waag at Haarlem (Fig. 82) in the north—no real parallels in the Netherlands before van Campen's Koymanshuis in Amsterdam and his Mauritshuis in The Hague, both of the second quarter of the century as has already been mentioned. Exception must be made, all the same, of Rubens's friend Wencelas Coebergher's remarkable *Basiliek* at Scherpenheuvel, northeast of Brussels near Aarschot, which was begun in 1609 and completed in 1627.[155] That round church, however, is already almost more early Baroque than Academic, at least as regards the facade. Like Giovanni Trevano's facade on the Jesuit church at Kraków in Poland of 1605–19, this follows contemporary Roman models much more closely than did the Jesuits at Antwerp and their architect P. Huyssens in the slightly later Sint Carolus Borromeus–kerk of 1614–21.[156]

No early date for the initiation of the reaction against Northern Mannerism can be set as definitely as in contemporary Germany or in England; but change had begun by the end of the first decade of the century in the Netherlands as it had—at least episodically—elsewhere in northern Europe. Hendrick de Keyser's Waag of 1609 (Fig. 89) at Hoorn in Noord Holland, though relatively modest in size, offers a particularly sharp contrast to such buildings of the immediately preceding years as Opbergen's late masterwork at Gdańsk (Figs. 91, 92). Neophyte as he was at Academic design de Keyser,[157] without being able actually to rival the Haarlem Waag's very advanced character, doubtless did intend to emulate it in this stone structure of identical purpose. He would have known, as modern scholars do not, whether the older architect, Lieven de Key, had actually been responsible for its design. But he would have eschewed on principle by this date the Northern Mannerist detailing of de Key's Vleeshal in Haarlem of 1602–3 (Figs. 85, 86) and his earlier Leiden Raadhuis (Figs. 78, 79). Except for the hip roof and the rather widely spaced windows of vertical oblong shape in the upper storey on the long side, there are few specific resemblances, only a general similarity in the scale, the tone, and—perhaps most significantly—in the consistent use of stone laid up as smooth ashlar.

Used as an alternative to rustication or the more northern chip-carving, the ornamented blocks in the imposts of the Hoorn Waag and the similar ones that provide the voussoirs of the arches are hardly Academic, though the ground storey does recall a little the rusticated arcading on such an already mentioned public structure in another part of Europe as the slightly earlier Rathaus in Luzern—a work not likely to have been known to de Keyser! The upper windows, except for their spacing, are almost of vernacular character with plain wooden mullions, transoms, and painted shutters. However, the bracket-like keystones of the flat arches of the upper windows sound a more Academic note. These also provide support, in a rather un-canonical way, for the continuous and boldly projecting cornice. That cornice, more than any other element here, contrasts with the long-established Netherlandish habit of capping facades with decorated gables. Some suggestion of the familiar sort of gable survives, however, in the gablets of the dormers. The arches with carved voussoirs on the dormers echo those of the ground storey, but the sides still have scrolling if of a very restrained sort. Nor are the pediments capped by spike-crowned balls a novelty, even if more dominant in scale here than before.

Dating from 1611, two years after the Hoorn Waag, there is a house facade at Wester-straat 125 in Enkhuizen, like Hoorn in Noord Holland, that better illustrates the dichotomy of Dutch architectural design at this point. Because of the consistent use of an order in the upper storey, as two years later at Bolsward, this facade could be considered somewhat transitional, but otherwise it is still characteristically Northern Mannerist. The plain ground storey was evidently rebuilt, most probably in the late seventeenth or eighteenth centuries. The upper storey, between the pilasters, has three exceptionally broad and nearly square windows, two of them repeated at smaller scale in the lowest stage of the gable. About this modest facade three things are especially striking: the closely set stone banding in relief; the bossy projection of the ornamental motifs—not at all typically Vredemanesque but recalling a little that on Opbergen's Gdańsk Arsenal (Fig. 91)—and the heavily scaled scrolling at the edges of the gable. Excessive, indeed, all three of these things may seem on a facade of such small dimensions, but for that reason all the more unmistakably Northern Mannerist with no flavor yet of Academic restraint.

Of precisely the same date as the Bolsward Raadhuis are two other town halls that also survive, neither of them very advanced in character. On the modest one at Graft in Noord Holland all the three gables are still stepped and one of them, in any case, was rebuilt in the restoration of 1909. That at Hoorn (Fig. 94) is larger and also more interesting. From the front nothing is visible of the medieval Convent of Saint Cecilia the authorities had taken over for secular use. But on the street there rise paired gables, basically of the stepped sort though with minor scrolling atop the steps. The architect-builder made the most of the awkwardly bent street front as an Academic architect would hardly have done. The entrance projects, all in stone, at the break in the facade plane and, above between the two big gables, there is on the same center line a sort of blind gable boldly, even coarsely, scrolled which is much smaller. This is capped with a lion, while the big gables carry allegorical figures above the segmental pediments that crown them.

As with Lieven de Key's Vleeshal of ten years before in Haarlem (Figs. 85, 86), what is most conspicuous in the design of the Hoorn Raadhuis is the profuse use of stone inserts as alternate quoins on vertical elements and as alternate voussoirs in the broadly splayed flat arches over the stone-mullioned and transomed windows. Only the single windows in the second stage of the gable are arched. The delicate fluting that fills the lunettes within these arches contrasts with the heavy scale of the other features of the facade.

Of rather different character, more consistently scrolled and not so vigorously bichromatic yet not at all Academic, was the tall gable on the *Hof van Nassau* at Arnhem, dated 1614. That did not survive the last war, but is known from a photograph at the Kunsthistorisch Instituut in Utrecht of a modern measured drawing. The equally tall, but much more elaborate, four-staged gable with the date 1616 over the *Weeshuis* facade in the Westerstraat at Enkhuizen is only a modern copy; it is best appreciated in an old drawing of the original (Fig. 95). The three-sided "arches" over the windows in the lowest stage of the gable, especially as associated here with rather stubby paired pilasters, were a popular motif in these years. Such were used even by Rubens on his Antwerp house, but that is neither typically Northern Mannerist nor plausibly Academic.

The earliest examples of three-sided arches in Holland would perhaps be those on the lower storey of the *Rasphuis* in Amsterdam, thought to date from about 1603 and attributed to Hendrick de Keyser. Its two-stage gable was a clumsy confection that need not be illustrated. With its coupled pilasters, it seems to have been little more than an ignorant attempt to emulate Academic design, by no means up to de Keyser's later Waag at Hoorn in intrinsic quality. Quite similar to the Enkhuizen Weeshuis, but with a consistently scrolled three-stage gable, is the one in Edam, also dated 1616, which survives intact. The three-sided arches, the paired pilasters, and even the segmental arch in the gable could once be matched on the upper storey and the three-stage gable of the contemporary, or slightly earlier, *Huis St. Rochelle* in Amsterdam.

Of the following year, 1617, is the facade of a small house at Westerstraat 158 in Enkhuizen (Fig. 96), rivaled in pretension only by the earlier one of 1611 at No. 125 in the same street. Again there are three-sided arches in the upper storey as on the contemporary Weeshuis, but this facade owes its striking character, very like that of the earlier house in Enkhuizen, to the bold banding of the wall surfaces. In the first and second stages of the gable there are paired pilasters, but any tendency toward Academic restraint is contradicted by the size and prominence of the flanking scrolls. Ornament is largely restricted to the band over the big—and much later—windows of the ground storey and the tympana of the three-sided arches in the upper storey.

Even though that ornament is no longer typically Vredemanian, the total effect is still very Northern Mannerist. A much more transitional facade is that of the broad—today double—*Huis Bartholotti* at Herengracht 170–172 in Amsterdam (Fig. 97). This is thought to be a few years later in date, around 1620, and has been attributed to Hendrick de Keyser even though he died in 1621. Narrow brick pilasters, with tiny Doric capitals on the ground storey and Ionic ones above, divide the facade into bays; but the width of the bays varies slightly and there are solid half-bays at either side in the upper storey. The relative restraint of the bits and pieces of ornament, both in quantity and in size, is parallel to that of work which is more certainly of de Keyser's design, but there is still a three-stage gable above the center. Balustrades to left and right join the lowest stage of the gable to flanking niches, emphasizing the horizontality of the facade as a whole. These niches, two to a side, are framed by pilasters repeating the ones flanking the outermost windows of the storey below though their rhythm is looser. This treatment further parallels elements in de Keyser's known work, but the scale is naturally smaller here, as is appropriate to a house, than the scale of his contemporary Amsterdam churches. Only a faint flavor of Northern Mannerism survives in the ornament though the second stage of the gable is still flanked by scrolled members. However, the emphasis is again on the horizontal, and round urns on top of both of the middle stages of the gable now provide the recurrent terminal motif rather than the tall slim obelisks which had hitherto been so popular in northern Europe.

Several other facades of the early 1620s, though more retardataire, will shortly be described. These offer especially cogent examples of Netherlandish architecture in this transitional period. More consequent, however, is the fact that Academic design of a rather Palladian sort was at this point being introduced by Jacob van Campen in the Koymans Huis of 1625[158] at Keisersgracht 177 across from de Key's great Westerkerk, which was begun in 1620 but was still far from complete in 1625. On the broad facade of this house— eight bays wide against six on Huis Bartholotti—the pilasters are canonically detailed, with none of the minor bits of Northern Mannerist ornament introduced on the earlier one. Most notably, there is no gable at all but only such a straight entablature as had already crowned the Haarlem Waag in the 1590s. A variant of the Koymans Huis is the one at Herengracht 72. That, like the more palatial free-standing Mauritshuis in The Hague by van Campen and Pieter Post, is dated 1633.

In contrast to these initiatory Academic house-fronts in Amsterdam was once the modest facade at Kalverstraat 183 (Fig. 98) there. Dated 1624, this is known only from an eighteenth-century watercolor. By that decade simplified Northern Mannerist design had almost become a vernacular. This mode has a peculiarly Dutch—as distinguished from a more broadly Netherlandish—visual appeal. Examples still exist in quantity in the present-day Dutch townscape and can be appreciated even better in many old paintings of various cities as they were in the seventeenth century.

In contrast to this appealing near-vernacular of the early seventeenth century is the small, but pretentious, facade of what is now the Westfries Museum Hoorn, once governmental headquarters for the Noorderkwartier (Fig. 99). Except for its very vertical proportions and the profusion of carved work, this closely approaches the Academic as is not surprising considering the date, 1631–32. Pilaster orders in bold relief subdivide the two storeys below and the two stages of the gable above into bays—three of equal width below and in the lower stage of the gable a central bay, of the same width as those below, flanked by half-bays.

The orders are rather correctly detailed with triglyphs—though too widely spaced—in the entablature of the Doric order in the upper storey and a pulvinated frieze to go with the Ionic order in the first stage of the gable. If the herms, scrolled in their lower outline, flanking both stages of the gable are hardly Academic in flavor, the broken segmental pediment crowning the whole is an architectural motif by no means alien to advanced designers in the north in the early seventeenth century. It had already been used both by Jones and by Holl in the previous decade and may even be called early Baroque rather than late Mannerist.

The carving is almost entirely heraldic, including the arms of the seven cities of the Noorderkwartier, those of West Friesland, and also of the house of Orange. What makes the facade seem scrolled, or at least scalloped, in the usual Northern Mannerist way are the seven lions that support the shields of the cities. The original facade was of blue Namur stone, but in 1908–11 it was entirely rebuilt in a harder sort of gray stone. That goes far to explain the particular sort of coldness in the execution of the detail.

The facade of the Deventer Landshuis (Fig. 100) has nothing Academic about it beyond the detailing of the underscaled entablatures capping the three stages of the gable. Not pilasters but pilaster-strips of brick, striped and topped by rebated blocks of stone, separate big windows subdivided by stone mullions and transoms. Though the main portal is flanked by fluted Corinthian columns, the lower third of their shafts is carved with ornament in the Vredemanian way; characteristically Northern Mannerist also is the multiple S-scrolling used at the edges of all three stages of the gable. The date 1632 of construction is carved above the niche occupied by the statue of a soldier (?) in the topmost stage of the gable; but that stage seems to date largely from 1927–28 when the facade was restored, fortunately not so drastically as the one at Hoorn. This might well conclude the story as regards Holland.

Weissman's drawings of a series of gabled fronts of seventeenth-century houses in Amsterdam (Figs. 4, 101) include none dating from the decade of the 1630s. However, a gable of 1620 that he illustrates is not dissimilar to the one on the Deventer Landshuis, though the second stage of it is disproportionately tall compared to that on the facade, dated 1615, which is beside it in the drawing. By 1640, all the same, a new cycle seems to have evolved, one that represented a sort of uneasy compromise with the Academic. Thus, Dutch gables of the mid-seventeenth century are only nominally in continuation of the Northern Mannerist line of which the Deventer gable is about the latest full-blooded example. However, what is in some degree a prototype for the gables of the mid-century—a gable with pilasters flanking both stages and a plain pediment over the upper one—can be seen on a house in Weissman's drawing which is dated as early as 1594. That might seem like a direct descendant of certain gables of the 1540s here called Serlian (Figs. 29, 31). An intermediate step would be the gabled dormer on the front of the Amsterdam Paalhuis of 1560 (Fig. 44) which lacked, indeed, any major curved elements at the sides. Whether such gables of a century later should be considered Academic or Baroque is inconsequential. They are certainly outside the century-long line of Northern Renaissance scrolled gables to which this general account of Netherlandish work of the sixteenth and the early seventeenth century is devoted.

XI "Dutch" Gables in Early Stuart England

ALL THE SAME these later, somewhat Serlian, gables in Amsterdam do have a particular international interest. They may have been the inspiration, if not the actual models, for what are known in England as "Dutch" gables. Of these, John Summerson notes,[159] not a single example survives in London, though they can still be seen in quantity on the "Dutch House" of 1631 at Kew Gardens near London and a few years later at Raynham in Norfolk and at Swakeleys in Middlesex. The interesting questions have long been: When were such gables first used in London and what, specifically, were their foreign models? The earliest certain evidence comes from John Smythson, who saw on a visit to London in 1619 a house fronted with stone in Holborn which had lately been built for Sir Fulke Greville and two others, probably of brick, that were also in Holborn.

Of the Greville house and of one identified by him as "My Ladye Cooke's" Smythson made and dated drawings (Fig. 102).[160] Above the crowning entablature of the latter, echoed below by cornices over each of the two lower storeys, he indicates a single stage in the gable outlined by plain scroll-like bands of concave curvature linked together at the top and with coiled spirals at their lower ends. In the middle, a curious lambrequinlike bit of ornament, more or less Northern Mannerist in character, hangs down into the field. The field is also

95

cut at the base of the arch of a window rising over the central oriels of the lower storeys. There is nothing like the ornament on the Greville gable as drawn by Smythson or in the surviving project, sometimes associated with the Greville house, that is almost certainly by Jones himself (Fig. 103).[161] The most striking element of the Cooke gable is the heavily corniced segmental pediment above. However, Smythson's drawing shows the pediment on the Greville house as pointed; so does the project that has just been mentioned and illustrated. The gables at Raynham are similar and, even more, the ones at Swakeleys. Though the pediments capping these last are pointed, on the "Dutch House" (Fig. 104) the sides of the gables are S-curved, with the pediments segmental on the central one and pointed only over those at the sides.

Summerson has suggested that Nicholas Stone might have brought the concept of such gables with him from Amsterdam when he came back in 1613 to London, where they were recognized as being "Dutch." Actually, however, there were at that time few, if any, gables in Amsterdam or elsewhere in Holland closely resembling the ones drawn by Smythson in 1619 or that on the Jones project, which is thought to be of about 1616–17. Since roofs in the Low Countries were much higher and steeper than in London, gables in Holland were almost always taller also and more vertically proportioned. Above all, they were with few exceptions multi-staged. Yet Stone or some other English craftsman of the sort Summerson calls Artisan Mannerist could have borrowed, of course, only a lower stage from some gable in Holland—one that was horizontal in its broad proportions and flanked either by concave C-scrolls or by S-scrolls—finishing off the top, as often in Amsterdam, with a pointed or segmental pediment (Figs. 4, 101). From the first the combinations, as later on the "Dutch House" at Kew, were evidently thus varied. The relative simplicity of the concept and also the Academic flavor of the crowning pediments suggest a different source, one more plausible for Jones since it is Italian: no less than Serlio's gateway at the rear in his woodcut of 1545 of a *scena tragica* (Fig. 30). So also the side gables at Raynham, by their scale and their placing at the ends of the facade, are more reminiscent of the concave-sided ones over the wings of Palladio's Villa Barbaro at Maser than of anything in Holland, much as the temple-theme in the center of the garden front at Raynham recalls Palladio's there.[162]

The elevation (Fig. 103), thought possibly to be an early project for the Fulke Greville house, which survives among the Jones drawings at Chatsworth, does not resemble at all closely the Smythson drawing of 1619 of the Greville house as executed. The elegant character of the draftsmanship of the two main storeys and the attic of the facade seems close already to that of Jones's drawings of 1619 for the Prince's Lodging at Newmarket.[163] On the other hand, the freehand indication of the S-scrolls above is somewhat coarser. If this drawing precedes by several years 1619, as John Harris believes, it might well be the earliest English design for a "Dutch" gable. It would provide relevant evidence of an early Jonesian innovation unrelated—indeed, even opposed in character—to his major architectural work for English royalty beginning in 1616 with the commission for the Queen's House.

The suggestion that Jones may have been involved with the introduction of "Dutch" or "Holborn" gables in London in the second decade of the seventeenth century brings in, however, an alternative foreign source for the motif in Germany, one Harris is ready, at least in principle, to support.[164] "Dutch" is sometimes used, not as a translation of *nederlandsche*, but of *deutsch*—in America the German settlers in Pennsylvania are called "Pennsylvania Dutch."

Summerson eventually established in 1970 that Jones reached Heidelberg in 1613 when he accompanied the Elector Palatine Friedrich V and his wife Elizabeth, the daughter of the English sovereigns James and Anne, on their return to the continent and did not leave the party, as was earlier supposed, at Strasbourg.[165] He was certainly familiar, therefore, with the existing Schloss, whether or not he actually provided designs for the new wing there, called the *Englischer Bau*, of 1613–15.[166]

To judge from an early engraving,[167] the original gabled dormers on the Englischer Bau were fairly small and of a rather restrained character, though scrolled as well as pedimented. On the wing to the east, built for Friedrich IV in 1601–7 by Johann Schoch from Strasbourg, but not on the earlier *Ottheinrichsbau* of the late 1550s, pairs of very large and ornate gables still survive on both the south and the north sides. These must have been as conspicuous to Jones as they are to us today. If these or other similar German gables were the models for Jones's project at Chatsworth (Fig. 103), he certainly chastened the motif. On the *Friedrichsbau*, for example, the gables (Fig. 105) have a first rectangular stage decorated with a peculiar order and with statues of Friedrich's ancestors by the Swiss Sebastian Götz. The Chatsworth elevation shows, instead, a continuous attic the full width of the facade below the main entablature, which is cut by five square windows corresponding to the tall cornice-crowned ones of the storey below. These are quite unlike Schoch's pedimented pairs of windows flanked by carved members on the gables at Heidelberg.

The second stage—first in the Jones project—of the gables is the crucial one. Admittedly, the broad, almost horizontal S-scrolls in the elevation, which are related to the lower pitch of an English roof, look little more like the ones on the Friedrichsbau than the windows below. All the same, the spiraled lower ends and the break in the S-shaped members just above can be read as a simplification of Schoch's less continuous spirals and S-curves at Heidelberg. The restriction of surface decoration in the Jones elevation to a molding outlining the surface between the S-scrolls and a plain oculus parallels the substitution of an Academic pointed pediment for the statue-crowned *welsche Gebel* at Heidelberg.

This parallelism does not help to establish the date of the Jones drawing beyond suggesting, as do other considerations, that it was posterior to his return to England in 1615, nor does it at all strengthen the attribution to him. On the contrary, the presumption might rather be that after his return from Italy in 1615 Italian ideas would have dominated totally. As to the attribution, it can only be said that the design is too accomplished for Smythson; perhaps, if not by Jones himself as Harris firmly believes, it might have been made under his close influence by Isaac de Caus or some other associate for another house than Greville's.

Summerson supposes that "Dutch" gables continued in use not only during the Commonwealth but even into the early years of the Restoration. However, the initiation by Jones and Isaac de Caus of the Covent Garden project in 1631[168] surely marks the moment when they began to go out of fashion in London. In that first London square, echoing to a degree the Place Royale in Paris, gables whether pedimental or scrolled had no place over the continuous cornice line of the houses. The facades, moreover, while simple, were distinctly Academic in their restraint and proportions. Long before that, however, Jones could well have found inspiration for scrolled and pedimented gables in his copy of Serlio (Fig. 30) as some designers in the Netherlands—and also, it seems probable, at Dresden in Saxony—had done so long before (Fig. 29), if not in Heidelberg or elsewhere in Germany.

Although Jones is no longer thought to have been responsible personally for the design of Raynham,[169] but rather the mason whom Sir Roger Townshend, the owner, took abroad with him to see up-to-date Italian architecture, a reflection of Palladio's Villa Barbaro seems more likely there than dependence on any other continental model. If the idea for the gables goes back to Townshend's first intention of building at Raynham in 1619–22—the very years when Jones was already erecting the Banquetting House in Whitehall—that might very well mean the new concept of the "Dutch" gables in London, as introduced in the preceding years shortly after 1615, was Italian: partially Serlian, at least, if not Palladian! As with other aspects of Jones's style when emulated by others, his somewhat Serlian model was soon corrupted by Northern Mannerist proportions and detailing. It could have been the corruption that was seen as "Dutch," whatever that word actually meant to contemporaries, with the northern character of the decorative part emphasized by using the term of alien reference for the whole. That would have been a reversal of the semantic history of the Italian word *piazza* when taken into English.

XII   Major Danish Works of the Early Seventeenth Century

WHILE NO "Dutch" gables survive in England earlier than those on a few country houses of the 1630s (Fig. 104), the situation was very different in Denmark. Christian IV long outlived his sister Anne, James I's queen and Jones's client for the Queen's House at Greenwich, and faced no such revolution as brought his nephew Charles to the scaffold. He was involved, however—and none too successfully—in the Thirty Years' War in the late 1620s. Work on the Frederiksborg Slot at Hillerød (Fig. 90) had continued into the early years of that decade. But at Copenhagen Christian had also begun as early as 1606[170] to acquire land outside the city walls for a formal garden in the French style. The "house in the garden" he then erected was modest in size, no rival to the existing Copenhagen castle. Additions were carried out in 1613–14, and the principal tower in the middle of the southwest side was added in 1616. This is the Rosenborg Slot.

Rosenborg is almost as Dutch-looking as Frederiksborg but differs from contemporary work in Holland by its great height and complex massing. This includes a fourth, rather small, tower added in 1633 in the center of the southeast front, but the tower is by no means a dominant feature. It is the work of Hans II van Steenwinckel; but the Slot as a whole probably owes at least as much to the rather specific ideas of the king as developed and carried out by the royal master-mason Bertel Lange.[171]

Another Danish royal project was the rebuilding, beginning in 1631, of Slot Kronborg (Fig. 106) after the fire of 1629.[172] As noted earlier, Hans II van Steenwinckel was in charge down at least through a payment he received in 1636. That was for the doorway, largely of black marble, in the King's Chamber. The doorway is more High Renaissance than Mannerist in design—or, it may be better to say by this late date—Academic, despite a mixture of various imported materials and painted polychromy as well. An earlier doorway, all of ebony and dated 1627–28, by the king's joiner, Anton Meiding from Augsburg, is by contrast still thoroughly Northern Mannerist.[173] The work at Kronborg was completed by the time of Hans II van Steenwinckel's death in 1639. Although he was required by the king to respect the earlier work of the 1570s and 1580s by Opbergen and his own father, he left his mark on the Slot, for he raised the roof of the Great Hall, elaborated the gable over the chapel, and added a score of new dormers with stone-faced gablets.

An earlier and much more richly decorated gable than any of those at Rosenborg or at Kronborg is associated with a church, that on the royal chapel Christian added to the Cathedral of Roskilde beginning in 1613,[174] together with a reredos, a pulpit, and a royal pew in the interior, not to speak of the spires on the exterior of the church. A few years later—work began in 1619—Christian extended the Holmens Kirke in Copenhagen, which has somewhat less elaborate scrolled gables over the four arms.[175] The church was already being modified in the 1640s and the interior fittings date from twenty years later, with further alterations in the nineteenth century.

A finer church that has survived in pristine condition despite the fact that it is now in Swedish, not Danish, territory, is that at Christiansstad, Skaasne (Skaanie today). Christian had begun a new town on this island in 1614[176] as a regular rectangle surrounded by bastions. Like other outlying islands off the Swedish coast that he fortified, this was more fortress than colonial settlement. The Trefoldigheds Kirken, founded by the king in 1617,[177] has an exceptional plan that is symmetrical on both axes. There is a big tower at the west end but the east end, of the same width as the nave, has a scrolled gable and there are three more on each side. Those of the transept ends in the center are flanked over the aisles by somewhat narrower cross-gables parallel to the transept.

A much larger and grander many-gabled structure begun shortly after the Christiansstad church is the *Børsen* (exchange) in Copenhagen. Exchanges were generally sponsored by groups of merchants, but in this case it was the king who was the patron, as he was in these years of explorers such as Ove Giedde who founded a Danish trading post in Ceylon.

The architect of the Børsen was to have been Laurens II van Steenwinckel, but he soon died and his brother Hans II took over as master-builder and architect on a contract of May 4, 1619.[178] As a young man Hans II had been sent to Holland to be trained by Hendrick de Keyser. That was in 1602, the year de Key began the Vleeshal at Haarlem. Some ten years later, after his return to his native Denmark, he was working for the king at Frederiksborg and at Christiansstad, where he seems to have been responsible for the fortifications but not for the church.

Not surprisingly Hans van Steenwinckel's Børsen (Figs. 107, 108) resembles de Key's Vleeshal, but it is much, much larger. The very site seems Dutch, for the building stretches along a canal, with nineteen bays on either side of the center. The two ends have broad three-stage scrolled gables and incorporate monumental portals flanked by orders that rise through the lower stage of the gable. The treatment of the sides is simpler, with a three-stage gable three bays wide in the center and narrower staged gablets rising over every third bay.

Three master-masons or bricklayers are mentioned: Rollefinck, Morton Weichardt, and Geert Backmann. Vidt Kragen was the master carpenter, and as his contract concluded in 1622, it may be assumed the construction fell largely in the previous two years, 1620 and 1621. The most remarkable feature of the Børsen, with no Netherlandish antecedents, was the "Four Dragons" on top of the central lantern whose tails twist upward into a tall helical spire. This was presumably completed by 1625. In that year Ludwig Heidenritter received the last installment of the 600 Rd due him, and Anders Neilsen was paid "For 3 crowns, 3 Balls and 1 flag" that he gilded. Construction slowed down during the war years of the late 1620s, and the Børsen was not completed until 1640, the date over the later of the two end portals.

Although the Copenhagen Børsen rivals in size and elaboration such other major works of this terminal period elsewhere as Opbergen's arsenal at Gdańsk and the Frederiksborg Slot here in Denmark, it is less typical than private commissions for houses, of which a certain number survive in Denmark. In Copenhagen little is extant, but the twin-gabled house at Amagertorv 6 is a fine example dated 1616.[179] An even more notable house is that of the prominent merchant Jens Bang in Aalborg, called Sten Hus. This occupies a corner site and therefore has more gables—three on the main street, the Østeragade, and a broader one on the left end. The brick is yellow, not red, and there is a great profusion of carved sandstone detail. This provincial mansion, unrivaled in size and elaboration by any surviving houses either in the Netherlands or Gdańsk, may well provide the last illustration in this book (Fig. 109).

The date of the Sten Hus is 1623–24.[180] That date and the particular character of the detailing on the gables both suggest Hans II van Steenwinckel was not involved here. Through these years Hans was loaded by Christian with work in Copenhagen and at Frederiksborg, if not still on the churches that have been described above. The designer could have been, like this Hans, Danish-born, whether or not of a Netherlandish family, but perhaps with the advantage—again like Hans—of study in Holland. Or he could have been himself a Netherlander. In any case, the restoration of 1917–19 did not dilute the Netherlandish character of the scrolled gables nor their prime distinction as late but impressive examples of this major theme of the Northern Renaissance. Yet the Sten Hus was erected only a year before the new Academic phase of architecture in Holland got under way with the building of the Dutch-Palladian Koymans Huis in Amsterdam by Jacob van Campen.

Moreover, this was several years after proto-Baroque architectural design first appeared in the north in the house Rubens built for himself in Antwerp in 1613–17. It was also the time when the Jesuits' Sint Carolus Borromeus-kerk there had already been brought nearly to completion and Coebergher's Basiliek at Scherpenheuvel—even closer as regards its front facade to those of the new churches in Rome—was already far advanced. Thus the mid-1620s are, internationally, an appropriate point to end this book, though Christian IV in Denmark, even in later life, seems to have accepted only in a few interiors at Kronborg and Rosenborg[181] the new Academic sort of architectural design, the sort his sister Anne had sponsored so long before for the Queen's House at Greenwich. From Margaret of Austria a hundred years before to Anne, certain northern princesses rivaled Marie de Médicis, employer of de Brosse and of Rubens, as supporters of advanced design in architecture, if not patrons on the same scale as she in the field of painting. Whether Renaissance or Baroque, however, in the early seventeenth century the most supportive clients were still not royalty, but rising merchants such as Jens Bang, in the great northern ports from Antwerp and Amsterdam to Gdańsk.

Notes

Complete bibliographical references to books and other publications are provided the first time they appear. Later, short titles only are given. The locations of the fuller entries can be found under the authors' names in the Index.

1. Particularly advantageous for Amsterdam was the Twelve Years' Truce, 1609–21, with the Spaniards, especially as peace survived its end. Just before the truce was to terminate, the two later of Amsterdam's three great seventeenth-century churches were begun in 1620 to the designs of Hendrick de Keyser. Not altogether irrelevantly, it might be noted that it was also in 1620 that the English Dissenters we call Pilgrims left Leiden to go to North America.

2. K. Fremantle, *The Baroque Town Hall of Amsterdam*, Utrecht, 1959, provides the best account of seventeenth-century Dutch architecture in any language.

3. Neither of the principal authorities on later French architecture, Anthony Blunt and Louis Hautecoeur, gives more than passing reference to the squares of Arras. Doubtless they consider them Flemish rather than French as the city *was* Flemish down to 1640. See, rather, J. Boutry, *Arras son histoire et ses monuments*, Arras, 1890, p. 62. Boutry notes that as early as 1574 the construction of wooden houses in the Arras

squares was forbidden. There is also J. Lestocquoy, *Arras*, Colmar-Ingersheim, 1972, p. 42, who mentions another edict, of 1583, controlling the character of houses to be built in the squares.

4. References are hardly necessary concerning such well-known monuments as these squares in Paris and Charleville.

5. The relevant geographical area extends in northern Europe from present-day Belgium through Holland up into Denmark to the north and, in a wide swath, eastward across northern Germany to Poland and the Baltic coast. The "northern Netherlands" refers here to modern Nederland and the "southern Netherlands" to what is now Belgium. Within Belgium the province of Brabant, where Antwerp and Mechelen (Malines) lie, and the province of Flanders, where are Gent (Ghent) and Brugge (Bruges), both ruled by the Habsburgs, should be distinguished from one another, as also Liège, a quasi-independent prince-bishopric in the sixteenth century. Provincial designations are not

provided for the larger Dutch cities such as Amsterdam, Leiden (Leyden), and Haarlem, but only for relatively small places otherwise hard to find on maps.

6. J. Białostocki, *The Art of the Renaissance in Eastern Europe*, Oxford, 1976, pp. 74–75, ills. 279–282.

7. Discussed below in chapter VI.

8. For the names of cities, the forms actually in use today in the countries or regions of northern Europe have been preferred; however, versions more familiar to American and English readers are given in parentheses when place names such as Gdańsk (Danzig), here, or Brugge or Leiden, as in note 5, are first used. This applies particularly to the names of places like Mechelen (Malines) in the Flemish-speaking provinces of Belgium. French names are often resented by local inhabitants, who may even pretend not to understand them!

9. Discussed in H.-R. Hitchcock, [*German Renaissance Architecture*], now in preparation, without page or figure references. Most German monuments mentioned in this chapter and later are also described and illustrated in that forthcoming work. Individual citations are irrelevant as they cannot be to specific pages and figures.

10. References are only rarely given henceforth for architectural production outside the areas of strong Netherlandish influence. Białostocki, *Eastern Europe*, is the most available source for monuments in eastern Europe.

11. Not alone Catholics but Baptists, Lutherans, and other Dissenters suffered persecution from the dominant Calvinists in Holland.

12. M. D. Ozinga, *De Protestantsche Kerkenbouw in Nederland*, Amsterdam-Paris, 1929, tells the story in Holland. It is worth noting, specifically, that none of the three great early-seventeenth-century churches of Amsterdam has scrolled gables. J. Skovgaard, *A King's Architecture*, pp. 78–86, being in English, is useful for the Danish churches of the early seventeenth century which do have such gables. Elsewhere in the north of Europe, outside the German lands, very few churches of the period survive with or without scrolled gables. The German churches will be discussed and many of them illustrated in Hitchcock, [*German Renaissance*].

13. Relevant in this connection is C. Wilkinson, "The New Professionalism in the Renaissance," in S. Kostof, *The Architect*, New York, 1977.

14. Reproduced by Parent, *Pays-Bas Meridionaux*, pl.

opp. p. 20, who gives the date as 1550. P. J. Goetghebuer, *Choix des monumens, édifices et maisons les plus remarquables du royaume des Pays-Bas*, Gent, 1827, is Parent's source.

15. L. H. Heydenreich and W. Lotz, *Architecture in Italy 1400–1600*, Harmondsworth, 1974, p. 16.

16. *Op. cit.*, pls. 115, 122.

17. *Op. cit.*, pl. 148c.

18. *Op. cit.*, p. 273.

19. E. Unnerbäck, *Welsche Giebel*, Stockholm, 1971, pp. 11–12, fig. 9.
    Albrecht began to order sculpture in Mainz for his Halle church in 1523: *Deutsche Kunstdenkmäler, Provinz Sachsen Land Anhalt*, Munich, 1968, p. 366. The Italian sources of the German gables would seem to be Venetian, perhaps specifically the Scuola di San Marco: H.-R. Hitchcock, "The Beginnings of the Renaissance in Germany 1505–1515," *Architectura*, 1971, no. 2, pp. 123–147; 1972, no. 1, pp. 3–16.

20. H. Kreft and J. Soenke, *Die Weserrenaissance*, 3d ed., Hameln [1969], pp. 276–278, fig. 234.

21. The subject will be discussed recurrently and elaborately illustrated in Hitchcock, [*German Renaissance*]. For a generous roster of fine photographs of scrolled gables in the district of the Weser valley, where German production climaxed in the decades 1580–1610, see Kreft-Soenke, *Weserrenaissance*.
    Unnerbäck, *Welsche Giebel*, gives the most space to various German districts from Westphalia and Hesse to Pomerania and East and West Prussia. Two terminal sections, pp. 60–76, deal with Denmark and Sweden. In Denmark German influence on architecture, as illustrated especially in gable design, was superseded, from the 1570s, by Netherlandish influence, beginning with the employment by Frederik II of Anthonis van Opbergen at the Kronborg Slot. The results of this are discussed at some length and illustrated in chapters IX and XII of this book. There seems to have been no parallel change in Sweden, though scrolled gables of more Germanic inspiration are not infrequent down well into the mid-seventeenth century.

22. Though a rather small city today, Mechelen remains the seat of the primate of Belgium as arranged with Rome by Philip II for Cardinal Granvella in 1559.

23. Actually begun in 1517 and most probably completed by 1526. Baedekers Autoreiseführer *Benelux*, 4th ed., Stuttgart [1967/68], p. 213, is the latest reference; but see also P. Clemen, *Belgische Kunstdenkmäler*, Mu-

nich, 1923, II, p. 18, of fifty years ago. Lemaire, *Gids*, p. 198, gives the basic dates for the structure as 1507–17 putting, however, the *Vroogrenaissance* (early Renaissance) wings as late as c. 1530.

The dating of many architectural monuments in Belgium is uncertain. In the crucial case of the north facade of the Palais de Savoie—better referred to in present-day Belgium as the *Gerechtshof*—Leurs in Duverger, *Nederlanden*, p. 60, gives 1535 as the date of completion. Since Margaret of Austria, for whom the work was certainly begun, died in 1530 and Beaugrant left Mechelen to go to Spain in 1533, this seems much too late.

24. The Emperor Maximilian's daughter Margaret of Austria—more properly known as Marguerite de Savoie—was made viceroy of the Netherlands by her father after the death of her brother Philip the Fair in 1506. She had been the widow first of the heir to the Spanish thrones, Carlos, and then of Philibert the Fair, duke of Savoy.

25. Horst, *Renaissance in den Niederlanden*, pp. 19–35, relates the churches mentioned here to the earlier phase of *Sondergotik*, for which see K. Gerstenberg, *Deutsche Sondergotik*, Munich [1913]. E. Hempel, *Geschichte der deutschen Baukunst*, 2d ed., Munich [1956], still devoted twice as much space, pp. 209–281, to the Sondergotik as to the Renaissance, pp. 282–329!

26. The completion of the chapel at Westminster was Henry VIII's responsibility in execution of Henry VII's will. King's College Chapel in Cambridge and St. George's Chapel at Windsor were also both completed by Henry VIII early in his reign. Another of his major benefactions was the Renaissance screen of the 1530s in the Cambridge chapel. Precise dating is, in the present context, not relevant.

27. The dates of these French monuments need not be referenced since they are generally accepted.

28. *Kunstreisboek*, pp. 570–574. Since most of the dates for Dutch buildings are drawn from this one most useful source, they have rarely been further referenced below. Many dates, however, appear on the buildings themselves, though they are not easy to make out in the illustrations.

29. Lemaire, *Gids*, p. 170. The shank of the tower was begun in the early fifteenth century. Construction of the spire started nearly a hundred years later. Several others were involved before Rombout Keldermans and Domien de Waghemaekere, notably the latter's father Herman. Domien was in charge 1502–30, Rombout from 1521. That date for the completion is surely too early. In any case, the professional association of Keldermans and Waghemaekere in Gent in these years suggests a parallel situation here.

30. The article in Thieme-Becker on the Keldermans family includes this Rombout, II; his father Anthonis I; and his brother Anthonis II.

Articles in Thieme-Becker are henceforth referenced only as "Th.-B.," but only those that are signed or, like this one, especially long and detailed are cited. Many are drastically out of date, especially, of course, for artists whose names fall early in the alphabet.

31. Lemaire, *Gids*, p. 184. The Raadhuis is the subject of an unpublished Gent University thesis by Dr. F. Dambre-Van Tyghem, who confirmed the basic dates in correspondence. The core of the structure dates from the late fifteenth century, the Bollaertskamer (Fig. 70) from the early 1580s, and the east wing mostly from after 1600 (Fig. 83). The whole was restored under Viollet-le-Duc's direction in 1869–70. The drawings, of which one is illustrated here (Fig. 71), are preserved in the Bijloke Museum in Gent.

32. Leurs, *Bouwkunst in Vlaanderen*, p. 53, gives the dates as 1515–31; A. G. B. Schayes, *Historie de l'architecture en Belgique*, Brussels, n.d., II, pp. 295–296, as 1514–23. Lemaire, *Gids*, p. 178, gives the dates of reconstruction as 1873–87 with no architect named.

33. Otto von Habsburg, *Charles V*, New York, 1929. E. Crankshaw, *The Habsburgs*, New York, 1971, pp. 57–77, is more objective, the author not being a descendant of the subject! Neither offers much on Charles's building activities in the Netherlands.

34. Lemaire, *Gids*, p. 197. The tower carries the date 1546. The craftsmen responsible for the stained glass were Antonis Everts and Claes Matuijs.

35. Baedeker, *Benelux*, p. 212. Lemaire, *Gids*, p. 189, gives the date as 1526–29, Schayes, II, p. 299, as 1530, with 1913 for the ultimate completion.

36. G. Fehr, *Benedikt Ried*, Munich [1961].

37. The *Epitaph* of Jacques de Croy (Jakob von Croy) dates from 1518: *The Treasury of Cologne Cathedral* (Art Guide No. 970), 2d ed., 1974, p. 22, ill. p. [24]. Croy, though a canon of Cologne, was a member of a Netherlandish family, and bishop of Cambrai when he died in 1516: [G. Dehio] Handbuch der Deutschen Kunstdenkmäler, *Rheinland*, Munich, 1967, p. 322. Von der Osten-Vey, *Painting and Sculpture*, pp. 57–58, suggests the gilded bronze edicule was cast, very likely at Louvain (Leuven) rather than Mechelen, and by Hieronymus Veldener, though from a design by someone else.

38. On reaching his majority in 1515 Charles V became

duke of the Netherlands under his grandfather Maximilian; but first Maximilian and then Charles, after his succession as emperor in 1520, retained Margaret as stadholder until her death.

39. G. Kubler and M. Soria, *Art and Architecture in Spain and Portugal . . . 1500 to 1800*, Baltimore [1959], pp. 10–11, fig. 6; Th.-B. article "Pedro Machuca," signed "L.S." [Scheewe].

40. Th.-B. article "Sebastiaan van Noyen" by M. D. Ozinga. Parent, *Pays-Bas meridionaux*, pl. opp. p. 20, reproduces elevations from early-nineteenth-century plates based on drawings by P. J. Goetghebuer that make very evident the High Renaissance character of this mansion. He gives the date as 1550. See Note 14.

41. Von der Osten-Vey, *Painting and Sculpture*, pp. 238–239.

42. Th.-B. article "Louis van Bodeghem" by H. Hymans.

43. Th.-B. article "Jan van Roome"; von der Osten-Vey, *Painting and Sculpture*, p. 145.

44. Th.-B. article "Conrad Meit" by Dorothea Stern; von der Osten-Vey, *Painting and Sculpture*, pp. 30–31, 238–40—a bust by Meit in the British Museum may be of Margaret and another of Philibert, *op. cit.*, pl. 218.

45. The accepted dates are 1523–24, but the screen may have been first commissioned some years earlier: [Dehio] *Rheinland*, pp. 358–359.

46. A. Blunt, *Art and Architecture in France 1500–1700*, 2d ed., Harmondsworth, 1970, p. 8.

47. Th.-B. article "Guyot de Beaugrant" by E. de Taeye. Parent, *Pays-Bas meridionaux*, assumed Guyot was a "sculpteur bressois," i.e., from Bourg-en-Bresse; F. O. van Hammée, *Mechelen*, Amsterdam, 1949, p. 67, calls him a "savoyard," which means much the same.

48. Th.-B. article "Lancelot Blondeel" by H. Hymans; von der Osten-Vey, *Painting and Sculpture*, p. 241.

49. Von der Osten-Vey, *Painting and Sculpture*, p. 240.

50. H.-R. Hitchcock, "The Beginnings of the Renaissance in Germany," *Architectura*, 1971–72, I, pp. 123–147.

51. I. Büchner-Suchland, *Hans Hieber*, Munich, 1972.

52. J. Z. Łozinski and A. Miłobedzki, *Guide to Architecture in Poland*, Warsaw, 1967, pp. 115–116; B. Knox, *The Architecture of Poland*, London [1971], pls. 10–13. Białostocki, *Eastern Europe*, provides a wealth of illustrative material, including a colored plate, that need not be cited in detail here.

53. Blunt, *France 1500–1700*, pls. 12a and b.

54. Gables are rare in French sixteenth-century architecture. By exception, the Francis I wing of the chateau of Amboise has one. This is a plain triangle crossed only by two string-courses. What is relevant at Amboise, as will shortly be evident, are the richly decorated stone dormers along the sides (Fig. 14). It is of incidental interest, but not probably relevant, that Margaret had spent her childhood in France at the chateau of Amboise.

55. Built 1445–51: Blunt, *France 1500–1700*, p. 14

56. *Op. cit.*, p. 9, pl. 7.
    It is worth recalling that in the last years of his life, 1516–19, Leonardo da Vinci lived outside Amboise as Francis I's guest and was engaged in designing the chateau of Romorantin. The Amboise dormers certainly do not derive from his church project of c. 1515, however, and no scrolled gables were proposed for Romorantin, though a tower does have something approaching a *welsche Gebel* at the top: C. Pedretti, *Leonardo da Vinci: The Royal Palace at Romorantin*, Cambridge, Mass., 1972, pls. 167, 168.

57. Blunt, *France 1500–1700*, p. 8, pl. 3.

58. J. Summerson, *Architecture in Britain 1530–1830*, 3d ed., Harmondsworth, 1970, pp. 31–32, fig. 6.

59. Th.-B. article "Pietro di Torrigiano di Antonio" by W. Gramberg.

60. Th.-B. article "Jacopo de' Barbari" signed P. K.; von der Osten-Vey, *Painting and Sculpture*, p. 59.
    Margaret's patronage included more Flemish and German artists than Italians; her employment, in addition to Lancelot Blondeel, of such northerners as Gerard David, Jan Gossaert (Mabuse), Jan Mostaert, Leonard Magt, and even Hieronymus Bosch is documented. Some of them, as well as the Italian Jacopo de' Barbari, were already employed by her brother Philip the Fair; von der Osten-Vey, *Painting and Sculpture*; others had entered her service long before in the 1490s, pp. 156, 161. This Habsburg support of art in the Netherlands tapered off after 1530 under Charles V's sister Mary of Hungary, who succeeded Margaret as stadholder and left Mechelen for Brussels.
    What is most relevant here is the fact that Margaret's northern artists, most of them at least, used Renaissance architectural elements in their paintings in some profusion.

61. Th.-B. article "Tommaso di Andrea Vincidor" by H. V[ollmer]. Vincidor left the Netherlands in 1527 to go

back to Rome, but returned in 1531 when he entered the service of Hendrick of Nassau. Torrigiani went on too early to England to have been involved.

62. If these features are, indeed, interpolations, they could be of 1535. That is when Leurs believes the north facade, as one could put it, was "reconstructed." See Note 23. But a date nearer the mid-century, as suggested earlier, would seem more likely stylistically. Certainly they do not resemble the work of this decade in Brugge (Fig. 25) or Liège.

63. P. Mazzola, *La Cattedrale di Como*, Rome, 1939.

64. F. Loeffler, *Das alte Dresden*, Dresden, 1955, pl. 34.

65. Blunt, *France 1500-1700*, pp. 9–12, pl. 7. No precise dating seems to have been established for the François Ier wing at Amboise, but it must have been erected in much the same years as the wing at Blois. It was certainly begun only long after Margaret had left when her marriage to the Dauphin was annulled.

66. A. L. J. Van der Walle, *De gotiek in België*, Brussels [1972], pl. 60; Lemaire, *Gids*, p. 188.

Dr. Dambre-Van Tyghem states in a letter that the Metselaershuis was originally at the corner of the Cataloniëstraat and the St.-Niklaasstraat. In 1852 it was demolished and the facade reërected on the Graslei when a storey was added. The relevant gable was not modified, or so it would seem.

67. Lemaire, *Gids*, gives the name of the builder as Christoffel van de Berghe and notes that the facade was restored in 1906. Dr. Dambre, in correspondence, corrects the date to 1530-31.

There is also an unscrolled gabled facade in Mechelen of uncertain date that can be considered transitional, though it does not at all reflect the later wings of the Palais de Savoie. Known as *Het Hemelrijck*, this house in O. l. Vrouwstraat has been dated by Castyne, *Architecture privée*, p. 104, "vers 1520," and by others as much as a decade or two later. It is well illustrated by Vandevivere, *Renaissance Art in Belgium*, p. 48, pl. 40, who gives the date as 1530-40. The lower stage of the gable is flanked by convex volutes and the upper is a plain *welsche Gebel*. The vertical elements in both stages are still Late Gothic, but the lunettes over the windows at all levels, alternately half-round and pedimental, are filled with ornament of rather *quattrocento* character. Perhaps there were once other similar gabled facades, decorated but unscrolled like this; the design, however, seems on the whole more Germanic than Netherlandish.

68. *Kunstreisboek*, pp. 546-548.

69. M. D. Ozinga, "Die strenge Renaissancestijl in de Nederlanden naar de Stand von onze tegenwoordige Kennis," *Bull. van de Kon. Ned. Oudheitsbond*, 6th series, XV, 10-34. Ter Kuile, in Rosenberg *et al.*, *Dutch Art and Architecture*, pp. 222-223, dates the initiation of the outer works at Breda "before 1521" though he offers no supporting documentation.

70. Floris van Egmond had been Henry VIII's representative among the trio of guardians Margaret of Austria selected for her nephew Charles in 1513. Floris's heiress, Anna van Buren, later married the Dutch stadholder, William of Orange-Nassau, known as William the Silent. He was the successor to Hendrick of Nassau-Breda after the death of his cousin René, Hendrick's son, who had made him his testamentary heir. René was the first Dutch prince of Orange as heir of his mother, Claude de Chalon-Arlay, who had inherited the Principality of Orange on the death of her brother Philibert de Chalon.

71. Not everything here is so correct: The Doric entablature of the lower order is extravagantly broadened to reach up to the sills of the windows in the next storey and the upper order has paired scroll-brackets between the capitals and the entablature. The general effect is Bramantesque, all the same, and the detailing of such a feature, novel in the north, as the straight staircase rising in two flights between walls most convincingly Italian.

72. One may well query whether these are of Vincidor's original design or entirely by Dutch craftsmen working in the years between his death in 1536 and Hendrick's in 1538.

73. In a letter de Barsée confirmed the date 1553 and provided relevant references, most notably to F. Smekens, *Stad Antwerpen, Oudkundige Musea, Het Brouwershuis . . .*, Antwerp, n.d., which includes a bibliography. Lemaire, *Gids*, p. 171, gives the date as c. 1555, however.

74. In his letter de Barsée offers the date "even na 1541," with references to Schayes, *Histoire*, p. 483; to Leurs, *Bouwkunst in Vlaanderen*, p. 527; and to his own *Antwerpen die Scone*, pl. 9, as well as several others.

75. Clemen, *Belgische Kunstdenkmäler*, II, p. 149; Lemaire, *Gids*, p. 198, dates it 1530-34.

76. Leurs, *Bouwkunst in Vlaanderen*, p. 59, gave the dates as 1530-35 in 1946, but he later seemed uncertain in Duverger, *Nederlanden*. The dates used in the text seem more probable and are now generally accepted: Lemaire, *Gids*, p. 175.

77. Th.-B. article "Christian Sixdeniers" by Marguerite Devigne.

78. Early knowledge in the north of Sanmichele's Palazzo Bevilacqua in Verona is surely unlikely, even though that was at least partially completed by the mid-1530s: Heydenreich-Lotz, *Italy 1400–1600*, pp. 217–218, pl. 224. The date, c. 1530, Lotz says, "can only be determined on stylistic grounds."

79. Lemaire, *Gids*, p. 194.

80. Timmers, *Dutch Life and Art*, pl. 262.

81. Dr. Dambre–Van Tyghem has confirmed the correctness of this date in correspondence. It is, in any case, visible in the illustration, if not very legible.

82. M. C. Laleman, "De ontwikkeling van het Gentse huisgeveltype in de tweede helft van de 16de eeuw," *Vlaanderen*, no. 153, July–August 1976, pp. 207–217, illustrates all the houses mentioned, with several more as well, and gives such dates as are known.

83. A. Horn and W. Meyer, *Die Kunstdenkmäler von Schwaben*, V: *Stadt- und Landkreis Neuburg an der Donau*, Munich, 1958, pp. 191–264.

84. *Op. cit.*, figs. 104–105.

85. *Op. cit.*, figs. 197–198. The arabesque decoration in terra cotta on the window frames of the north wing includes a medallion portrait of Ottheinrich and the date 1537.

86. An early prototype is provided by Alberti's scrolls on Santa Maria Novella in Florence as was mentioned earlier: Heydenreich-Lotz, *Italy 1400–1600*, p. 33, pl. 21. The theme is well represented on other Italian church facades of the 1480s and later: See their pls. 50, 105, 115, 148c. It may, therefore, have been known to Pasqualini before he came north.

87. Blunt, *France 1600–1800*, pp. 42–43.

88. Th.-B. article "Willem van Noort" by M. D. Ozinga; [H. E. van Gelder] *Guide to Dutch Art*, The Hague, 1961, p. 79.

89. Loeffler, *Alte Dresden*, pp. 18, 349. The accepted dates for the Grosser Hof (Moritzbau) are 1547–56, but work may have begun shortly after Moritz's accession as duke in 1541. Moritz became elector of Saxony only in 1547.

90. Parent, *Pays-Bas meridionaux*, pl. XIII.

91. Von der Osten-Vey, *Painting and Sculpture*, pp. 196–200.

92. Th.-B. article "Cornelis II Floris" by B. C. K. Von der Osten-Vey, *Painting and Sculpture*, pp. 279–281, deals chiefly with Floris's activity as a sculptor.

Some of the crestings, as in Fig. 34, might almost be considered scrolled gables even though they were of openwork with no roofs behind, as later atop the towers of Wollaton in England.

93. The publication was a production of the painter and book designer Pieter Coecke (1502–50), who was born at Aalst between Gent and Brussels: See Th.-B. article "Pieter I van Coecke van Aelst" by E. Plietsch. According to von der Osten-Vey, *Painting and Sculpture*, p. 196, he had originally "delivered or directed" the entrée. They also state that "He seems to have been the first Flemish artist to have taken up strapwork and grotesques [paving] the way for the first Floris style."

Coecke had published Vitruvian texts in Antwerp in 1537 and 1539, and later brought out Serlian texts there in Dutch, French, and German.

94. Van Gelder, *Guide to Dutch Art*, pp. 83–84.

95. Łozinski-Miłobedzki, *Guide to Architecture*, p. 75; Knox, *Architecture of Poland*, pp. 110–111, pl. 141.

96. Van Gelder, *Guide to Dutch Art*, p. 79. The dates supplied by the Rijksdienst voor de Monumentenzorg, Zeist, are 1551–56. An eighteenth-century drawing of the Bushuis survives but does not make the detailing of the upper stages any clearer than the photograph. The draftsman was evidently more interested, like the photographer, in the later and grander facade to the right, not to speak of the groups of figures in the street.

97. Von der Osten-Vey, *Painting and Sculpture*, p. 366, give references in their notes 5 and 7 to various early-twentieth-century publications concerning Floris's ornament and, more generally, *rollwerk* (bandwork) ornament of the sixteenth century in the north. The most up-to-date is E. Forssman, *Säule und Ornament*, Stockholm, 1956.

In any case, Floris's architectural style is ambiguous, whether or not he was responsible for the Antwerp Raadhuis. His executed work, including the framework of the tombs he executed in Germany and elsewhere, usually exemplifies what can be called Northern High Renaissance. On the other hand, the ornamental designs he published in 1556–57, though some reflect what he had seen on an Italian visit and also parallel the new sort of decorative detail already developing at Fontainebleau, represent a personal and idiosyncratic sort of Northern Mannerism. This seems to be distinctly his own, at least in its ripest state, even if the mode had been initiated in Antwerp by Pieter Coecke before Floris took it up. At this sort of ornament, however, others would eventually be more inventive than he, particularly Jan Vredeman.

98. Lemaire, *Gids*, p. 171, writes, "onder de leiding van Cornelis Floris," only.

99. R. Hootz, *Bremen Niedersachsen*, Munich, 1963, pl. 211, p. 386.

100. The date was supplied by the Rijksdienst voor de Monumentenzorg, Zeist.

101. Van Gelder, *Guide to Dutch Art*, p. 79.

102. Lemaire, *Gids*, p. 171, gives the dates as 1561–65. Some others say 1560–64. Von der Osten-Vey, *Painting and Sculpture*, p. 366, note 5, supply references to several articles relevant to Floris's responsibility for the design of the Antwerp Raadhuis as executed; in any case he definitely won the preceding competition. Lemaire notes that the Raadhuis was restored and drastically remodeled internally in 1855–69. The brown-and-white marble ashlar of the ground storey is of this date as the high polish suggests, and probably also the columns above of the same marble. The choice of this material was doubtless determined by what had survived; the interiors, however, are wholly of an elaborate nineteenth-century Neo-Renaissance character that can hardly resemble at all closely what was there originally.

103. The prominence and the profusion of the sculpture certainly seem to indicate that Floris was directly involved in the execution of the Raadhuis, whether or not he was alone responsible for the design.

104. Th.-B. article "Hans Vredeman de Vries [*sic*]" by Irmgard Koska. Neither Northern Mannerist ornament nor, more particularly, scrolled gables monopolize Vredeman's published designs it should be noted.

105. Von der Osten-Vey, *Painting and Sculpture*, pp. 281–282, give 1555 as the date of Vredeman's earliest published plates of ornament. They also mention his employment outside the Netherlands at Aachen, Wolfenbüttel, Hamburg, Gdańsk, and Prague. In Białostocki, *Eastern Europe*, ill. 320, is of his mural, the *Allegory of Lawful and Unlawful Behavior*, dated 1593–94, which is in the Red Room of the Town Hall of Gdańsk.

106. *Kunstreisboek*, p. 469, states the old castle at Woerden was demolished in 1559.

107. Kreft-Soenke, *Weserrenaissance*, pp. 251–253, 284–285, 291–303.

108. This consists of what appear to be two houses side by side facing on the Sint-Verle-Plein. It is not identifiable today as a former hospice. The date was supplied by the Bild-Archiv Foto Marburg that provided the photograph, but without reference to any Belgian authority. Laleman, in *Vlaanderen*, July–August 1976, p. 206, gives no date, but pairs the illustration of it, fig. 21, with fig. 22 of a house dated 1565 in the Lange Munt in Gent.

109. Łozinski-Miłobedzki, *Guide to Architecture*, p. 76.

110. *Op. cit.*, p. 75.

111. The date of the Amsterdam Burgerweeshuis was supplied by the Rijksdienst voor de Monumentenzorg, Zeist, which provided the photograph.

112. G. Piltz, *Kunstführer durch die DDR*, Leipzig [1973], p. 304.

113. Kreft-Soenke, *Weserrenaissance*, p. 20.

114. K. Goettert, *Das Kölnische Rathaus*, Mönchen Gladbach [1959], pp. [9–11], pls. [51–55]; Th.-B. article "Wilhelm Vernukken" by H. Vogts.

115. Th.-B. article "Alexander Colin" by Hans Tietze; B. Kossmann, *Der Ostpalast . . . zu Heidelberg*, Strasbourg, 1904, pp. 19–22. Colin's fame derives chiefly from his work, from 1562 onwards, in the Hofkirche at Innsbruck, related to the tomb of the Emperor Maximilian. According to the Th.-B. article, he returned to Mechelen several times in 1559, 1566, 1576, and 1599.

116. Piltz, *Kunstführer*, p. 470.

117. *Op. cit.*, p. 475.

118. Białostocki, *Eastern Europe*, ill. 316. Another major commission of Floris in the north is the tomb of Christian III of Denmark at Roskilde. This was executed in Antwerp over the years 1569–76 for Frederik II: Skovgaard, *A King's Architecture*, p. 85.

119. M. Backes, *Hessen* [Munich] 1966, p. 451; Th.-B. article "Elias Godefroy" by R. A. Pelzer.

120. R. Klapheck, *Die Meister v. Schloss Horst im Broiche*, Berlin, 1915. Klapheck's study, extending to 390 pages and profusely illustrated with photographs of surviving portions of the Schloss at Horst and others, nineteenth-century drawings, and twentieth-century paper restorations, must be the most extended single monograph on any German Renaissance Schloss not excluding Heidelberg. It provides as well much comparative material on related structures, not only nearby in Westphalia, but in the Netherlands and in France. For the most relevant section of the author's

attempt to describe and illustrate what once existed, see pp. 44–54; for those sections that deal with the architect Arndt Johannssen and his assistants, particularly Laurentz von Brachum, see pp. 66–84.

For the Schloss at Frens, see pp. 233–246.

121. Łozinski-Miłobedzki, *Guide to Architecture*, p. 76.

122. *Loc. cit.*

123. Kreft-Soenke, *Weserrenaissance*, pp. 247–248.

124. Hootz, *Niedersachsen*, p. 369; pl. 103 shows the Emden Rathaus as restored since World War II. For Laurens van Steenwinckel and his architect relatives see note 126.

125. C. Christensen, *Kronborg Frederik II's Renaessanceslot . . .* , [? Copenhagen], 1950, with English translation pp. 183–212; Skovgaard, *A King's Architecture*, pp. 14–21; Slothouwer, *Nederlandsche Renaissance in Denemarken*, pp. 62–119.

126. Skovgaard, *A King's Architecture*, pp. 131–132, gives biographical data on no less than five Steenwinckels; see also Slothouwer, *Nederlandsche Renaissance in Denemarken*, pp. 22–43, for the Steenwinckels. Skovgaard largely supersedes Slothouwer, but the latter's illustrations are useful.

127. *Op. cit.*, p. 15.

128. *Op. cit.*, pp. 75–77.

129. Baedeker, *Belgium*, p. 181, gives 1516 as the original date of construction, but notes that the facade was completely rebuilt around 1580. It has also been restored twice in this century in the 1920s and in the 1950s. L. De Barsée, in a letter, provides the dates 1579–82 and gives several references, most notably A. Thys, "La Maison Grande Place, 17," *Recueil des Bulletins de la Propriété publiée par le journal L'Escaut*, Antwerp [1883], pp. 118–120.

130. Another somewhat earlier gabled house in England, dating probably from the 1570s, is Trerice in Cornwall, but its central polylobed gable looks more Germanic than Netherlandish since it is not scrolled. The scrolled gables over the projecting wings that flank the facade are of wholly exceptional character and seem to be quite original here with no dependence on specific continental precedent: N. Pevsner, *Buildings of England: Cornwall*, Harmondsworth, 1970, article "Trerice," pl. 52. He gives the date as c. 1572. The National Trust, which owns the house, considers the date to be 1573—which is carved on a chimneypiece—and the builder as Sir John Arundell: R. Fedden and R. Joekes, *The National Trust Guide*, New York,

1974, pp. 206–207. Arundell had been in the Netherlands but none of his gables are "Dutch," even in the special English sense of those on London houses of nearly two generations later (Figs. 97–98).

131. Summerson, *Britain 1530–1830*, pp. 67–69, fig. 31; M. Girouard, *Robert Smythson . . .* , London [1966], pp. 77–95, figs. 30–43.

132. The rear extension was carried out for Sir Christopher Tatton in total disregard of the design of the court. He acquired the property after the death in 1575 of the original owner. That owner had begun the house in 1570, when the seven-year-old John Thorpe is recorded as having laid the cornerstone! What Tatton built at Kirby probably ran parallel with the construction of his other Northamptonshire house, Holdenby, which was completed in 1583. At Holdenby only two garden gateways survive, and their crowning medallions carved with Tatton's arms and the date 1585 are quite unlike the Kirby gables. Tatton, it may be noted, became Queen Elizabeth's lord chancellor in 1587: N. Pevsner, *Buildings of England, Northamptonshire*, Harmondsworth, 1961, articles "Holdenby" and "Kirby." For Holdenby, see also J. A. Gotch, *Early Renaissance Architecture in England, 1500–1625*, 2d ed., London, 1914, p. 92, fig. 80. For Kirby, see J. S. Carl, "Elizabethan Oasis," in *The Architect*, September 1971, pp. 60–61.

133. F. van Tyghem, "De Bollaertskamer," *Vlaanderen*, 153, July–August 1976, pp. 218–221.

134. M. C. Laleman, "Joos Roman en Lieven de Key," *Vlaanderen*, 153, July–August 1976, pp. 222–223.

135. Van Gelder, *Guide to Dutch Art*, p. 84.

136. The date was supplied by the Rijksdienst voor de Monumentenzorg, Zeist, together with the photograph.

137. Łozinski-Miłobedzki, *Guide to Architecture*, pp. 75, 77. Later sculptures from the St. James Gate of 1633–34, for which the Gdańsk city architect Jan Strakowski who succeeded Opbergen was responsible, were added in 1886.

138. The medieval tower was rebuilt in 1599, and the first extension of the facade followed in 1604. There were several later extensions and restorations: *Kunstreisboek*, p. 436; Th.-B. article "Lieven Lievensz. de Key."

139. Kreft-Soenke, *Weserrenaissance*, pp. 232–234. It is unsettled whether Bentheim had, in Bremen, any important part either in the design or in the execution of the decorative stonework on the Rathaus, of which

140. Th.-B. article "Willem Willemsz. Thybaut" by M. D. Henkel.

141. *Kunstreisboek*, p. 359; von der Osten-Vey, *Painting and Sculpture*, p. 337.

142. Dr. Dambre-Van Tyghem has confirmed the dates of the extension of the Gent Raadhuis in correspondence.

143. Reclams Kunstführer, *Schweiz und Liechtenstein*, Stuttgart [1966], pp. 435–436; R. Hootz, *Kunstdenkmäler in der Schweiz*, Munich, 1969, I, pl. 136.

144. *Kunstreisboek*, p. 145.

145. Skovgaard, *A King's Architecture*, p. 41.

146. *Op. cit.*, pp. 45–60; Slothouwer, *Renaissance in Denemarken*, pp. 89–119.

147. Other building projects of Christian IV were crowned with Dutch gables, notably the Rosenborg Slot on the outskirts of Copenhagen, a smaller edition of Frederiksborg, which was built piecemeal from 1606 to 1633. Hans II van Steenwinckel "was responsible for part of the work, especially the late stair-tower [of 1633] but the major part of Rosenborg was probably the work of the King and Bertel Lange his master-mason": *op. cit.*, pp. 67–74. There is also the Copenhagen Exchange of 1620–40 (Figs. 107, 108) with its endless arrays of gabled dormers along the sides. This was probably projected by Laurens II van Steenwinckel just before his death in 1619, but executed by his brother Hans II over the years 1620–40: *op. cit.*, pp. 87–91.

148. Kreft-Soenke, *Weserrenaissance*, pp. 236–237, pl. 201.

149. Łozinski-Miłobedzki, *Eastern Europe*, p. 75.

150. *Loc. cit.*

151. *Op. cit.*, p. 111.

152. *Op. cit.*, p. 75.

153. J. Summerson, *Inigo Jones*, Harmondsworth, 1966. Summerson's *Britain 1530–1830* of 1970, Part II, "Inigo Jones and his Times (1619–1660)," to some extent supersedes the earlier monograph.

154. There is an extensive literature concerning Holl. His work will also be discussed at length and illustrated in Hitchcock, [*German Renaissance*].

155. Baedeker, *Benelux*, pp. 84–85.

156. *Op. cit.*, p. 132, for Scherpenheuvel; Knox, *The Architecture of Poland*, pl. 14, for the Polish church.

157. E. Neurdenburg, *Hendrick de Keyser*, Amsterdam, n.d.

158. Fremantle, *Town Hall of Amsterdam*, p. 108, note 2 and *passim*.

159. Summerson, *Britain 1530–1830*, pp. 100–101, 157–160.

160. J. Harris *et al.*, *The King's Arcadia*, London, 1973, pl. 189. Smythson indicates a width of only three bays for the Greville house as executed; the project preserved at Chatsworth has five (Fig. 103).

161. In a letter accompanying a photograph of this Chatsworth drawing John Harris noted that both in "Inigo Jones and the Courtier Style," *Architectural Review*, July 1973, and in *The King's Arcadia* he accepted "without hesitation that the Chatsworth gable design [Fig. 103] is wholly by Jones." He continued: "In terms of draughtsmanship it should be compared with the theatre K[ing's] A[rcadia] pls. 194, 195, which [he, i.e., Harris, has] almost certainly identified with Jones's design for the Phoenix Theatre in Drury Lane, opened in 1617."

162. Summerson, *Britain 1530–1830*, pp. 160–161, ill. 114–115.

163. J. Harris, "Inigo Jones and The Prince's Lodging, Newmarket," *Architectural History*, II, 1959.

164. To quote Harris from his letter again (see note 161), he specifically states: "And I agree with you that Jones got the gable idea from Germany." He further remarks: "We must remember . . . that Jones was travelling, probably through France, Germany and Italy, between 1598 and 1601. I [Harris] now have almost certain proof he was in Copenhagen in 1603 because among the dinner guests of [the king] Christian IV was a Mr. Johns, which must be Jones. Therefore in 1603 he must have spent a considerable amount of time observing the northern gable brick style . . . subsequently he was again subjected to it on the 1613–15 travels."

165. Summerson, *Britain 1530–1830*, p. 116. Harris in his letter gives the dates of the week Jones spent in Heidelberg as June 7–14. He then took nearly a month to reach Basel on July 9. Harris further remarks: "We are, of course, plagued by the big question mark as to whether Jones had time to make little side trips from his main route [via Strasbourg]. Could he have gone to Augsburg? I think he might have done. . . ." There, for example, he could have seen such an example of

advanced proto-Academic design in Germany as the *Stadtmetzg* (butchers' guildhouse) of 1609, whether that was designed in the years immediately preceding this date by the Swiss-born Joseph Heintz, who died in that year, or by Elias Holl, who executed it. While by no means a necessary model for the 1616–17 project, it is at least closer in spirit, if not in detail, than the Friedrichsbau at Heidelberg or anything in Holland up to this time.

166. See Hitchcock, [*German Renaissance*].

167. M. Merian, *Die Schönsten Schlösser, Burgen und Gärten*, Hamburg, 1965, pl. 36.

168. Summerson, *Britain 1530–1830*, pp. 134–137.

169. *Op. cit.*, pp. 157, 160, and fig. 114.

170. Skovgaard, *A King's Architecture*, pp. 67–74.

171. H. Langberg, *Hvem byggede hvad*, Copenhagen, 1952, I, pp. 335–337, gives Willum Cornelissen or Laurens II van Steenwinckel as possible architects. There are monographs on Rosenborg by B. Luisberg, 1914, and V. Wanscher, 1930, he notes.

172. Skovgaard, *A King's Architecture*, pp. 75–77.

173. *Op. cit.* illustrates both doorways on p. 77.

174. *Op. cit.*, pp. 78–80, 85. The design of the Roskilde chapel may have been provided by the king himself. The contract of 1513 with Laurens II van Steenwinckel suggests that he was employed only to supervise the construction. That responsibility continued down to his death in 1619 when his brother Hans II took over.

At Roskilde there are two royal tombs, that of Christian III, of which Cornelis Floris executed the elements in Antwerp over the years 1569–76 as was noted earlier, and another of Frederik II (d. 1589) erected at Helsingør by the Netherlander Gert van Egen in 1594–98; for that a drawn project of 1574 survives. The spires were commissioned in 1633 and completed two years later: *op. cit.*, p. 85.

175. *Op. cit.*, p. 81.

176. *Op. cit.*, p. 103.

177. *Op. cit.*, p. 82.

178. *Op. cit.*, pp. 87–91.

179. *Op. cit.*, p. 95.

180. *Op. cit.*, p. 96: "Jens Bang, once so wealthy, lost a great deal of his fortune during the war of 1627–29 and may have been insolvent when he died."

181. *Op. cit.*, pp. 70, 77.

Illustrations

Fig. 1. Amsterdam in 1638. The entrée of Marie de Médicis

Fig. 3. Arras, Grande Place, seventeenth and eighteenth centuries

Fig. 2. Arras, Grand Place, sixteenth and seventeenth centuries

Fig. 4. Amsterdam gables, 1500–1620

Fig. 6. Rombout Keldermans and Domien de Waghemaekere, Gent,
Raadhuis from N.E., 1518–35

Fig. 10. Jan van Roome, Cologne, Sankt Maria-im-
Kapitol, Hackeney screen, 1523–24

Fig. 5. Halle-a.-d.-Saale, Dom, cons. 1523

Fig. 7. Rombout Keldermans and Domien de Waghemaekere, project for Raadhuis in Gent, elevation of gable, ?1518–19

Fig. 8. Anthonis I or II Keldermans, Mechelen, Palais de Savoie, court to S.W., 1507–15

Fig. 9. Anthonis I or II Keldermans, Mechelen, Palais de Savoie
from S.W., 1507–15

Fig. 11. Rombout Keldermans and Guyot de Beaugrant, Mechelen, Palais de Savoie, N. front, 1517–?26

Fig. 12. Rombout Keldermans and Guyot de Beaugrant, Mechelen, Palais de Savoie from W., 1517–?26

Fig. 14. Amboise, chateau, Francois Ier wing, c. 1515–24

Fig. 15. Gaillon, chateau, gatehouse, 1508–10

Fig. 17. Rombout Keldermans and Guyot de Beaugrant, Mechelen, Palais de Savoie, N. entrance, 1517–?26 (the coat of arms is modern)

Fig. 13. Lancelot Blondeel and Guyot de Beaugrant, Brugge, Vrij, 1528–30

Fig. 18. Gent, Metselaershuis, 1526

Fig. 19. Gent, Vrijeschippershuis, 1531

Fig. 24. Antwerp, Wewershuis, c. 1541

Fig. 16. Hans Knotz, Neuburg-a.-d.-Donau, Schloss, N. wing, 1535–37

Fig. 25. Jean Wallot and Christian Sixdeniers, Brugge, Griffie, 1534/5–37

Fig. 20. Alessandro Pasqualini, Breda, Kasteel, entrance to outer works, 1532, in an eighteenth-century drawing

Fig. 21. Tommaso Vincidor, Breda, Kasteel, court elevation, 1536–38

Fig. 23. Tommaso Vincidor, Breda, Kasteel, 1536–38, in 1743

Fig. 26. Gent, De Fonteine, 1539

Fig. 27. Hans Knotz, Neuburg-a.-d.-Donau, N. gable
on W. wing, early 1530s, as before 1824

Fig. 22. Tommaso Vincidor, Breda, Kasteel,
S.W. gable, 1536–38, in an
eighteenth-century drawing

Fig. 29. Alessandro Pasqualini, Buren, Kasteel, court, c. 1540, as in 1728

Fig. 28. Arnhem, Duivelshuis, 1540–46, as restored since
World War II

Fig. 30. Sebastiano Serlio, design for *scena tragica* in *Architectura*,
Segundo libro, 1545

Fig. 32. Zaltbommel, Jan van Rossum house, early to mid-1540s, before demolition

Fig. 31. Willem van Noort, Utrecht, Raadhuis, 1547, from an engraving of 1697

Fig. 33. Culemborg, Markt 11, 1549

La figure de l'eschaffaulx fur la Coepoortbrugge.

Haulteur
.lx. piedz.
Largeur
lxx.piedz.

Fig. 34. Cornelis Floris or Pieter Coecke, reviewing stand on the Coepoortbrugge, 1549, in *Triumphe d'Anvers*, Antwerp, 1550

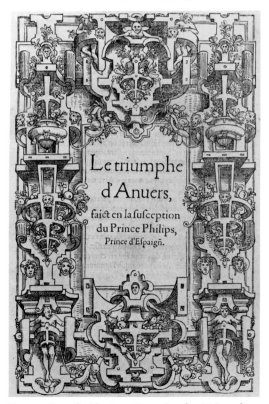

Le triumphe
d'Anuers,
faict en la fufception
du Prince Philips,
Prince d'Efpaigñ.

Fig. 35. Cornelis Floris or Pieter Coecke, *Triumphe d'Anvers . . .*, Antwerp, 1550, title-page

Fig. 36. Zierikzee, Stadhuis, 1550–54, elevation

Fig. 37. Amsterdam, Bushuis, 1555

Fig. 38. Cornelis Floris, plate from *Weeldeley Niewe Inventien van Antycksche*, Antwerp, 1557

Fig. 39. Haus Twickel, near Delden, 1557

Fig. 40. Edam, Weeshuis, 1558, from an eighteenth-century drawing

Fig. 42. Zierikzee, Noordhavenpoort, 1559

Fig. 41. Groningen, Kardinalshuis, 1559, before restoration

Fig. 43. Enkhuizen, Waag, 1559

Fig. 45. Cornelis Floris, Antwerp, Raadhuis, 1561-65, E. front

Fig. 46. Cornelis Floris, Antwerp, Raadhuis, 1561–65, gable

Fig. 44. Amsterdam, Paalhuis, 1560, from an eighteenth-century watercolor

Fig. 47. Jan Vredeman de Fries [*Architectura*, Antwerp], 1563, title-page

Fig. 48. Jan Vredeman de Fries [*Architectura*, Antwerp], 1563, pl. 146

Fig. 51. The Hague, Raadhuis, 1564–65

Fig. 50. Gorinchem, Huis Bethlehem, 1566

Fig. 49. Gent, Wenemaerhospital, 1564

Fig. 54. Regnier and Johann Kramer, Gdańsk, Zielona Brama, 1563–68, W. front

Fig. 55. Amsterdam, Burgerweeshuis, 1560, as in
1725

Fig. 53. Gdańsk, Długa, 37, 1563

Fig. 52. Gdańsk, Długa 45, c. 1560

Fig. 56. Erfurt, Roter Ochse, 1562

Fig. 59. Johann Kramer, Gdańsk, "Lion's Castle," Długa 35, 1569

Fig. 57. Arndt Johannssen or Laurentz von Brachum, Horst, Schloss, gable in court, early to mid-1560s

Fig. 58. ? Arndt Johannssen or Laurentz von Brachum, Schloss Frens, S.E. gable (late seventeenth-century copy of N.E. gable of c. 1565)

Fig. 60. Hoorn, Sint-Jansgasthuis, Boterhal, 1563

Fig. 61. Leeuwarden, Kanselarij, 1566–71

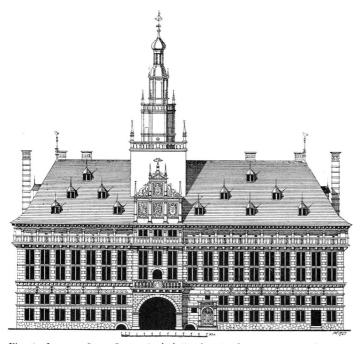

Fig. 62. Laurens I van Steenwinckel, Emden, Rathaus, 1574–76, elevation

Fig. 64. Kasteel Cannenburg, near Vaassen,
tower on front, ? c. 1570

Fig. 63. Hans van Paschen, Anthonis van Opbergen, Hans I and Hans II van Steenwinckel, Helsingør, Kronborg Slot, begun 1574; 1577–c. 1590; restored after fire 1631 ff.

Fig. 65. Deventer, De drie Haringen, 1575

Fig. 66. Antwerp, Oude Voetbooggildehuis, 1579–82

Fig. 68. Kirby Hall, Northants., rear wing, c. 1575–83

Fig. 69. Kirby Hall, Northants., gable, c. 1575–83

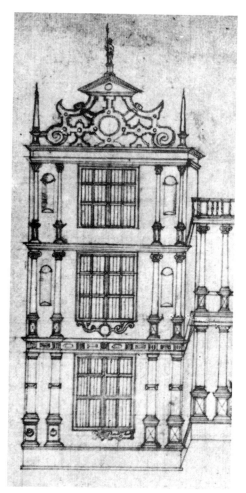

Fig. 67. John Thorpe (Robert Smythson), partial
elevation of Wollaton Hall, Notts.,
1580–88

Fig. 71. Joos Rooman, Gent, Bollaertskamer, 1580–82, watercolor of 1585 by Lieven van der Scheiden

Fig. 70. Joos Rooman, Gent, Bollaertskamer, 1580–82

Fig. 74. Andries de Valkenaere, Middelburg, In de Steenrotse, 1590, as restored without a gable

Fig. 73. Middelburg, Sint-Jorisdoelen, 1582, as restored c. 1970

Fig. 75. Deventer, Penninckshuis,
c. 1590

Fig. 72. Alkmaar, Waag, front, 1582; tower, 1597–99

Fig. 79. Lieven de Key and ? Lüder von Bentheim, Leiden, Raadhuis, 1594–99

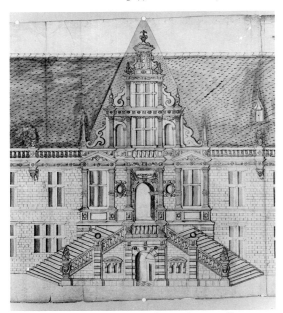

Fig. 78. Lieven de Key, project for Leiden Raadhuis, 1594

Fig. 76. Franeker, Raadhuis, 1591–94

Fig. 80. Lieven de Key, project for Gemeenlandshuis van
Rijnland in Leiden, 1597

Fig. 81. ? Lieven de Key, Leiden, Gemeenlandshuis
van Rijnland, 1597–98

Fig. 84. Arnhem, Rijnstraat 41, c. 1600 (Zeist)

Fig. 77. Anthonis van Opbergen, Gdańsk, Więzienna
Tower, 1587

Fig. 85. Lieven de Key, Haarlem, Vleeshal, 1602–3, front

Fig. 82. ? Willem Thybaut and Cornelis Cornelisz., Haarlem, Waag, 1597–98

Fig. 86. Lieven de Key, Haarlem, Vleeshal, 1602–3, side

Fig. 83. Gent, Raadhuis, extension, 1595–1618

Fig. 89. Hendrick de Keyser, Hoorn, Waag, 1609

Fig. 87. Nijmegen, Kerkboog, 1605

Fig. 88. Amsterdam, Stadbushuis, 1605

Fig. 90. ? Hans I van Steenwinckel, Caspar Boegendt, Hans II and Laurens II van Steenwinckel, Hillerød, Frederiksborg Slot, 1601–c. 1615

Fig. 91. Anthonis van Opbergen, Gdańsk, arsenal, 1602–5, E. front

Fig. 95. Enkhuizen, Weeshuis, 1616, from a
nineteenth-century watercolor

Fig. 93. Jacob Ghijsberts and Maarten Domenici, Bolsward, Stadhuis, 1613–17

Fig. 92. Anthonis van Opbergen, Gdańsk, Arsenal, 1602–5, W. front

Fig. 97. ? Hendrick de Keyser, Amsterdam, Huis Bartholotti, c. 1620

Fig. 94. Hoorn, Raadhuis, 1613

Fig. 99. Hoorn, Westfries Museum, 1631–32, as rebuilt

Fig. 96. Enkhuizen, Westerstraat 158, 1617

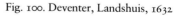

Fig. 98. Amsterdam, Kalverstraat 183, 1624

Fig. 100. Deventer, Landshuis, 1632

Amſterdamſche · Gevels.

Fig. 101. Amsterdam, facades with scrolled gables, 1640–1740

Fig. 102. London, Holborn, Lady Cooke's house,
elevation as drawn by Robert Smythson in 1519

Fig. 103. Inigo Jones, house project, elevation, ?1616–17,
preserved at Chatsworth

Fig. 104. Kew, "Dutch House", 1631

Fig. 105. Johann Schoch, Heidelberg, Friedrichsbau, 1601–7

Fig. 107. Hans II van Steenwinckel, Börsen, Copenhagen, 1619–40

Fig. 109. Aalborg, Sten Hus, 1623–24

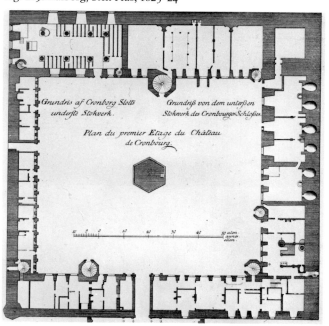

Fig. 106. Kronborg Slot, plan and court elevation as restored by Hans II van Steenwinckel, 1631–36

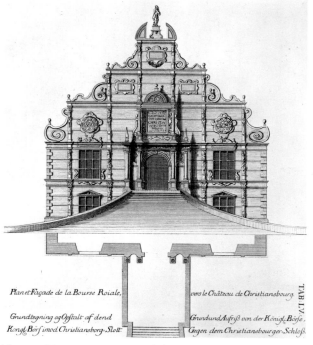

Fig. 108. Hans II van Steenwinckel, Börsen, Copenhagen, 1619–40, elevations

Index

DATE DUE
